POCKETS FULL

of

POSEYS

by A. J. Finn

DORRANCE
PUBLISHING CO
EST. 1920
PITTSBURGH, PENNSYLVANIA 15238

Dorrance Publishing Co
585 Alpha Drive
Suite 103
Pittsburgh, PA 15238
Visit our website at www.dorrancebookstore.com

ISBN: 979-8-8902-7169-3
eISBN: 979-8-8902-7667-4

To Gpa Posey, for showing me with a little determination and grit (and a couple beers) you can fix anything.

To Julia and Denise, a couple of ladies who showed me that the quality of your life isn't the cards you were dealt; it's how you play them.

And to Professor Severus Snape, for showing me that you can be dark and twisty and still have a heart of gold. Always. <3

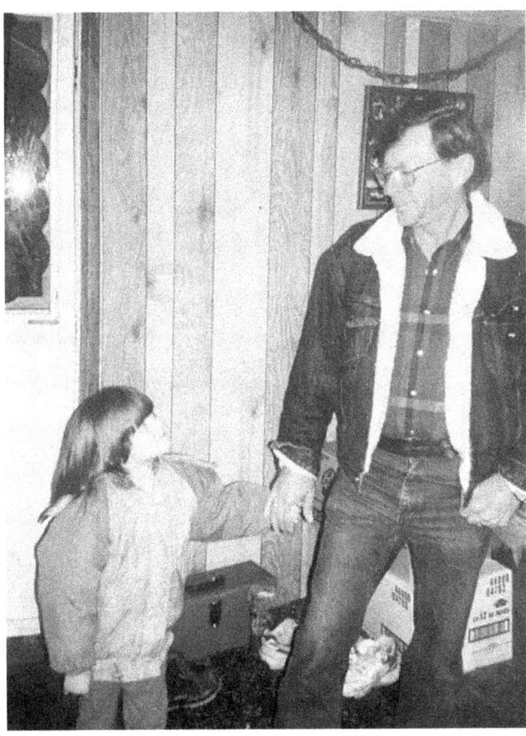

"Happiness can be found even in the darkest of times, when one only remembers to turn on the light."

—Albus Dumbledore

Contents

TRIGGER WARNING

This story is full of triggers, from domestic violence, sexual abuse, alcohol and drug use, murder plots, profanity, suicide, and eating disorders. And no, this isn't some rock band's tell-all; this is the story of my childhood, and while it is told in my voice there are other people's stories intertwined with mine that I will do my best to relay as I remember and as they pertain to my own story. Some names and dates have been tweaked to protect both the guilty and the innocent. If you aren't fluent in sarcasm, you might have trouble getting through this one. Read at your own discretion.

Preface

When I was in my twenties, I was never a fan of psychedelic drugs. I was more of a champagne and cocaine kind of girl. However, I had a hippie bestie who was into a more spiritual type of vibe. When she invited me to come take ayahuasca with her in Telluride, I shrugged. I've always been a big fan of peer pressure. It doesn't take much to get me running through fire for a good time. *Fuck it,* I thought to myself. *Try everything once.* I drove the seven hours to the remote mountain cabin she had sent me the address to. She instructed me to either fast the day of or eat something really clean, like a green smoothie or some toast. So naturally, I stopped at a Wendy's drive-thru on my way up.

As I pulled up to the modest mountain cabin, I wondered what exactly it was that I had signed myself up for. I walked inside and looked around. A small kitchen was off to the left side of the entryway. After the kitchen, it opened into a large main room with tall vaulted ceilings. The beams of unfinished exposed wood holding up the cabin still smelled like they had just been cut down from the woods outside. The main room was sparsely furnished with two beat-up couches and several camping chairs. I made my way to the nearest couch and after a short conversation about what I had for lunch, we drank the Kool-Aid, so to speak.

I had taken mushrooms a few times before this and knew how they tend to creep up on you, like a long, sweet romance finally coming to fruition with a forbidden love. I was expecting something similar. I'd soon learn that ayahuasca was nothing like mushrooms. Instead of a slow, sweet caress, it was more of a tsunami. It felt like getting body-slammed by John Cena in a wrestling arena. As the wall of the drugs I had taken bitch-slapped me, I started to realize that I was fucking in for it. After the initial impact, I was overcome by an overwhelming urge to vomit.

In a panic, I let myself out of the front of the cabin and started retching up my Jr. Bacon Cheeseburger onto a fresh snowbank. It was early spring. As I looked around me, wiping the vomit off my lips with the sleeve on my

Patagonia jacket, I realized I was in a different dimension. I'd never seen anything so beautiful. I leaned into the trip and took a deep breath. The crisp mountain air felt like an icy remedy to all my problems, each breath reincarnating my lungs that had been thrashed from years of vaping. Aspens around me grew arms and started chanting in unison for me to dance with them. I'm not much of a dancer, but it just felt right. The birds around us started chirping Ava Maria and the trees and I had a magical moment. With my arms spread wide, in full twirl, I suddenly realized I was about to shit my pants.

Thus, I made my way back into the cabin to find the nearest restroom. After that crisis was averted, I found my way back to my chair in the living room. I started seeing visions, flashing by my mind's eye too quick to grasp. Flashes of people I used to know ripped through me, piercing my soul in a "hey, maybe you shouldn't have broken up with him like that" kind of way. I tried to get them to slow down, as the room felt like it was spinning. Terrified, I started to imagine my soul breaking into a million pieces, like a snow globe being violently thrown against a wall. It felt like napalm was spreading into every nook and cranny of my entire being. I resisted the urge to vomit as I begged whatever bigger force was fucking with me to go easy on me. I wasn't spiritual enough for this shit. All of a sudden, everything slowed down. I took a few more deep breaths and realized I was looking at myself from the outside. All the horrible things I usually thought about myself not being enough aesthetically seemed to wash away in an instant. I realized I was actually kind of hot.

As I watched myself, a woman walked up to me. She looked like me, but different. At the time, I was rocking porn-star blonde hair with shitty tape-in extensions and wore an unholy amount of makeup. The woman had really short brown hair and no makeup. She grabbed my face in her hands and looked deep into my eyes. She said nothing, and all of a sudden the vision flashed to my father in a hospital bed. It then flashed to his headstone that read "June 2019." It flashed back to the woman holding my face in her hands.

"Do you have anything left you need to say, for you?" she asked me.

I opened my mouth to answer her, but no words would come out.

The woman released my face from her hands and walked me into a small room. Once inside, I realized that I was wearing a straitjacket. I looked around the room she had walked me into and was horrified to find it was a small cell with padded walls.

The woman looked at me and smiled reassuringly. "A. J., your mind is a prison and you're never gonna get out if you can't learn to let things go."

I tried to scream but nothing came out. She gently patted me on the shoulder and led me out of the room. I spent the next couple hours crying listening to music with my friend as the ayahuasca wore off.

The next morning, I drove back to Denver from Telluride. The whole drive back I thought about my father lying in a hospital bed. Did I have anything left to say? I never spoke about my childhood, and I certainly didn't speak to my piece-of-shit father. Really, the only thing I thought I'd like to do in my father's hospital room was use his pillow to smother him.

But I couldn't shake the padded room and the woman telling me my mind was a prison. How did I let this shit go? It was in that moment that I realized my story deserved to be told. And I promised myself that one day I would write a book about my fucked-up childhood. So buckle up, bitches, because I finally did it.

Chapter 1

Leaving LALA Land

Our story begins in the city of Los Angeles in the eighties. Amidst the neon colors and croon of Tears for Fears that seemed to echo out over the entirety of the sprawling metropolis, the city was bursting at the seams with the energy of people from all over the world, who had come there in search of some sunny Hollywood kind of vibes. The hair was big, the shoulder pads bigger, and the pants were tight, like really tight. At the time, my mother, Deb, was a bit of an awkward seventeen-year-old coming into her own. She had big glasses, perfectly permed reddish brown hair, and a good amount of underlying mental illness. She lived with her parents and three siblings outside the city. A true valley girl, she dreamed of a more exciting life and was looking to make her mark on the world. With a push-up bra and the bluest eyes the city of Los Angeles had ever seen, she set off to a house party one evening in search of a good time.

My father, Greg, was a twenty-eight-year-old illegal alien from Canada who had recently walked out on a wife and eighteen-month-old baby girl. He hopped that privacy hedge in the North and made his way down to LA in hopes of becoming an actor. In search of the American Dream, he found himself headed to the same house party that night. As he made his way to the party on his motorcycle, his perfectly quaffed hair blew in the wind. He listened to "Hotel California" on his radio as he sped down the 405. His knock-off Members Only bomber leather jacket was just decent enough to pass for authentic. My father was a great many not awesome things, but there was a time when he was a very attractive man. With a short athletic build, jet-black hair, and piercing green eyes, he exuded confidence in a devil-may-care kind of way.

Turns out, the two had both been invited to the party by the same mutual friend. Their eyes locked across the smoke-filled room as "Don't You Forget About Me" blared on a boombox in the corner. They walked toward each other in a trance and their whirlwind romance began, as they shared several lines of coke off of a mirrored-glass coffee table. I would love to tell you hopeless romantics out there that it was destiny that my father became a successful actor and my mother lived her best life and had a million perfect, beautiful babies. But I'm sorry, my friends, Jim Carrey was not my father. My parents' romance was more like a slow-motion train wreck that played out over the course of thirty years. It was the kind of terrible accident you don't want to look at but can't seem to look away from due to the battlefield level of carnage and smell of burning flesh our macabre human nature can't seem to resist.

While my father was trying to elbow his way into the upper echelons of Hollywood, he was also doing the same with my mother's family. My mother's two younger sisters were less than thrilled with my mother's new beau. They weren't seduced by his fake leather jacket and motorcycle. They knew she deserved better and wanted to protect their older sister from the predatory cradle-robbing vibes they had picked up on from my father. I'm sure the fact that he was living on a cot in the back of the gas station he worked at also contributed to their disdain. On one occasion, one of my aunts vandalized his motorcycle, pulling cords out and kicking it around a bit. But despite their best efforts, my parents were married on New Year's Day shortly after my mother's eighteenth birthday.

My older sister and I were born not long after. With her new set of Irish twins, my mother was quickly thrown into the role of a teen mother and homemaker. As she began drowning in motherhood and depression, my father began drowning in drugs and booze. My father had a love of brown liquor and a propensity for violence, which he began to take out on my mother shortly after they married. After a particularly nasty row, my mother fled with her black eye and bruised body to her brother's house, leaving us with my father. My uncle drove her back to our Moorpark home with a baseball bat and a plan: Get us from my father and help my mother escape. When they pulled up to the house, though, my mother lost her nerve. I do think she knew better than anyone what level of violence my father was really capable of. She wanted to be with her babies and she believed there was no way she would get us back from my father without us getting injured in the process. So she tucked tail and walked back in the house, where she would remain for the next three decades.

Deb must have realized that it was easier to stomach living with my father if she indulged in his vices with him, as she also began experimenting with heavier drugs that cocaine. With two small children and a gas station attendant's income, they were certainly balling on a budget. Crack quickly became a cheap alternative to their mutual love of cocaine. One particular evening, they got their hands on some meth. My father became enraged over something and got violent. My mother called her brother twacked out of her mind, and my uncle and grandpa raced to our home to see what was going. Needless to say, the chaos they observed led to my sister and me spending the evening at my grandparents' house. Shortly after this, my father decided it was time to get out of Dodge and perhaps get my mother a little farther away from her support system.

My father's acting career was short-lived. He worked as an extra in a few films and eventually landed a more permanent gig voicing a puppet dog in a very cheesy PBS sitcom loosely based on the exploits of Sherlock Holmes. After a few seasons, the show was ultimately canceled and my father had to find another income source. Due to his immigration status, it was difficult for my father to find legitimate work. Conveniently after his marriage to my mother, he was able to take a construction job in Texas. When that didn't work out, we ended up moving back up to Canada to try to make it work up there. We stayed in Canada for a few months, before moving down to Montana, where my mother had a good amount of family. Montana is where I started to have my earliest memories. Everything pre-Montana has been relayed to me by other characters in this story.

We lived in a rural logging town in Montana called Libby. The toxic wasteland riddled with asbestos dust from old mines seemed like an appropriate backdrop for the beginning of my childhood memories. A white doublewide trailer with purple trim was what we called home. My mother worked in daycares and my father drove a garbage truck for a short time. I started elementary school here, and it wasn't until I started elementary school that I realized how poor we actually were. My holey sneakers and oversized hand-me-down clothing led to some teasing from classmates. But despite living in poverty, Montana was where I had some of the happiest memories of my childhood. We lived a short distance from my aunt, cousins, various great-uncles, and my great-grandmother on my mother's side. We spent a good amount of time with relatives during this period of my life. My younger brother was born in Montana, and thus our family continued to grow.

I had my first experience with alcohol in Montana. My parents had a bunch of people over one night. There was a bonfire in the front yard, and all the kids were running around the trailer playing tag. I remember being parched from running around, so I ran up to a table and grabbed a bottle of clear liquid I thought was water and started chugging it. After a couple seconds, I realized that it wasn't water, but was instead some type of burning poison that the devil himself must have poured and set out on our table, also known as vodka. I spit the vodka out and started crying and all I remember is all the grown-ups bursting out in laughter like I had just told the most hilarious knock-knock joke ever. Needless to say, I don't remember much past that point that evening.

Memories are tricky things. Most of mine from childhood are fragmented and disorganized. I've spent a good many years and tens of thousands of dollars on therapy throughout my adult life, and one of the big take-aways I've learned about childhood memories is that a child's mind can dissociate from painful memories to protect the brain from the trauma. My memories have been loosened up over the years of EMDR and various forms of specialized therapy, but they are still a hot mess. They aren't necessarily in chronological order and neither is this story.

The same year as the vodka incident was when I started having dreams about my father climbing into my bed and touching me. I also started wetting the bed quite often around this time, which my father didn't have much patience for. My father was so upset about me wetting the bed that he took a cutting board with a handle from the kitchen and decorated it with markers, christening it "The Paddle." When any of us children got out of line, or in my case wet the bed, our father would wail on us with The Paddle. He would always note that we were very lucky that we didn't have his father, because his father used the belt, which was much worse, apparently.

I was always a stubborn and prideful child. Perhaps it's because I'm a Leo, or maybe it's because I ran out of fucks to give when I was five. Either way, it was around this time I started to realize my father got some sick satisfaction from hitting us until we cried. The seeds of hatred for my father had already been sown, so it became my life's mission to rob my father of any pleasure he reaped from hitting me. I would clench my teeth as I listened to the sounds of my sister's screams and imagine myself one day grabbing The Paddle and using it to bludgeon my father to death. I knew one day the tables would turn. And it seemed like I was the only woman in my family with the strength to defy my father. So when he would beat me from that point forward, I refused to cry, which ended up getting me a few extra whacks every time. Totally worth it. It wouldn't be too long before I stopped crying in general. These days, I average about two good cries a year, which I'm sure is totally healthy.

My great-grandmother's Montana home was a sanctuary for us children. Her house was a quaint folk Victorian that was tan with burgundy trim. She had a beautiful front porch that was decorated with vintage patio chairs and floral cushions. The inside was furnished with 70s-style furniture covered in plastic. Her floors boasted perfectly pristine orangish-brown shag carpet that she vacuumed daily, twice a day when she entertained company. Whenever we walked in her front door, we were greeted with the soft whisper of the scent of rose perfume and talc powder. All the windows in her home were adorned with suncrystal prisms that turned the daylight into magical rainbows. As a small child, I would run by the windows with my hands outstretched, trying to catch the beautiful rainbows and put them in my pocket.

My great-grandmother was born in 1918, during the Spanish Influenza pandemic. And believe me, she had seen some shit. She had survived the Great Depression, the Second World War, the Korean War, and the Vietnam War, as well as Richard Nixon's presidency. She had buried two husbands and one child in infancy. I overheard her telling my aunt one day that nothing could phase her, because she had no tears left to cry. I could certainly relate. Her frugality was something to be admired. I swear to God, that woman had the same roll of tinfoil for over a decade. She had cut the roll into the various sizes of all her casserole dishes. Once used, she would handwash them in the sink and hang them on her drying rack along with all her Ziplock bags. Whenever she went out to eat, she would snag two packets of Sweet'n Low and add them to her ever-growing collection of condiments.

Her backyard was the best part of her home. At the time, it seemed like the eighth wonder of the world. Although modest in size, it was a beautiful secret garden made up of various vegetables, rhubarb plants, huckleberry, and raspberry bushes. The true magic, though, was in the gooey smell of honeysuckle and the dozens of hummingbird feeders she had scattered all around her property. I would watch in awe as what seemed like hundreds of hummingbirds would flock around them, their tiny wings moving faster than anything I had ever seen. When they had drunk their fill, they would dart off into oblivion. I always wondered where those elegant creatures flew off to. I longed so badly to fly off with the hummingbirds and never return to my hellish existence.

I was quite close to my great-grandmother during our years in Montana. She was always kind to me and taught me to do a great many things. We shared the same birthday. And as a fellow Leo, I watched in awe as she would use her silent prowess to command each room she walked into. I used to want to be the first woman in the NFL and would steal her paper towel rolls and run around her house scoring touchdowns, which apparently annoyed the shit out her. But she took it all in stride. She taught me to crochet, make jellies, and mind my manners. She also taught me how to play cribbage, and we would play together for hours. During our cribbage games, she would gently tap on the table if my posture was anything less than ladylike. Perhaps all this is what has contributed to my generational identity crisis. I am a millennial but seem to identify as more of a boomer. My love of WW2 documentaries and "pull yourself up by your bootstraps" kind of outlook must have come from her. I do hate Facebook, though, so there's that.

Christmas Eve 1995 was the only time I ever saw her cry. My great-uncle, her son, blew his brains out with a shotgun on Christmas Eve right before he was supposed to come over for dinner. His funeral was the first one I attended. I sat on her lap the whole graveside service. I remember feeling her chest go up and down against my back as she stifled silent sobs behind me. My mother had told me that my uncle had been very sick and was in a better place now. I couldn't comprehend why everyone at the funeral had been so sad if he was in a better place. It wasn't until I was fourteen that she told me he had committed suicide.

The night of the funeral, I had a dream I was trapped in the cemetery my uncle was buried in and was trying to escape. The graveyard was covered in a thick coating of fog and an atmosphere of impending doom. I was being chased by wiggly cartoon-like skeletons. I kept running along a path until I ran into my uncle. I pleaded with him to help me escape. He gave me a flashlight and pointed down another path and told me the way out. I ran down the path until something grabbed me from behind and I dropped the flashlight he had given me. The dream ended with a flashlight spinning on the ground, and I woke up with a start drenched in sweat. I proceeded to have the same dream every few months for almost a decade until my mother told me about his suicide. It was then that the dream stopped.

Shortly after this, we moved quite suddenly to the eastern plains of Colorado. We had just gotten a brand-new Ford Explorer in the weeks before the move, so naturally I thought we had suddenly become rich and would be moving into a big beautiful house with a white picket fence and everything would be awesome. My big dreams about our new life in Colorado fizzled out upon our arrival about as quickly as my father's acting career.

Chapter 2

The Garden of Eden

Our arrival in Colorado was unceremonious and dismal. We drove a half-mile down a dirt road into a trailer park full of eight perfectly spaced-out single-wide trailers to our new home. The trailer park was also home to a few migrant Mexican families. When we first pulled in, I remember seeing a group of children running around the middle of the trailer park by the dumpsters. My father uttered a few racial slurs and then assured us we wouldn't be in that trailer park for long. We would remain there until my senior year of high school.

Pretty soon after our move, the Explorer would get repossessed. My grandparents had just bought me a new pair of black sneakers, which I had left in the car, not knowing that if you didn't make your car payments a couple men in reflective jackets could come into your life and take your car, sneakers and all. The repo happened while I was in school in that day. When I got home, my father was drunk as a skunk and my mother was washing dishes in the kitchen. I asked her where our car was and she told me we didn't have it anymore. Tears welled up in my eyes as I asked my mother if she had grabbed my sneakers out of the Explorer before they took it. She started to answer me and my father cut her off. "That's not our fucking problem, eh? That's what you get for being a fucking idiot." I said nothing and went to my room to mourn the loss of my black sneakers in privacy.

In Colorado, my father began to sip the Jesus Kool-Aid with a Jim Jones type of fervor. However, he was still sipping the Crown Royal a little harder, which led to a stark dichotomy between the times my father was on and off the wagon. When he was on the wagon, we were expected to be good little Christians, say our prayers, go to church, and always respect our parents. When he was off the wagon, we never knew what we'd be coming home from school to. Sometimes he was wasted and we would do our best to tiptoe around him and play outside until dinnertime. Sometimes he was out at the bar, and one time we came home from school to find he was in jail for assaulting a coworker on a construction jobsite. Needless to say, he was unemployed for a good while after this incident.

My understanding of Jesus as a young child was that he was a kind of like my fairy godmother and if I had a pure heart and asked him for anything, the world would eventually be mine, kind of like Cinderella. So I started asking him every night in my prayers to take my daddy to Heaven so he couldn't hurt us anymore. I prayed for this for quite some time to no avail. I decided it was time to take matters into my own hands, and thus the assassination attempts began.

My father by this time was pushing 350 pounds and seemed quite incapable of grabbing anything for himself. He would have my mother and us make him sandwiches, bring him beers, and generally do everything around the house because it was "women's work." My mother would work an eight-hour shift at a daycare and then come home to clean and cook with us for my father, who had spent the day funneling Crown Royal and salt-and-vinegar chips down his gullet.

One day my father told me to heat him up a plate of leftovers and suddenly a lightbulb went off in my mind. I slyly smiled my Grinch smile as I heated up his food in the microwave and proceeded to squeeze an entire bottle of Visine on his food. I handed him the plate, went back to my bedroom and waited for him to die. I do firmly believe my heart shrank three sizes that night. I braced myself for the few years in juvie that would surely be coming my way. I figured I would do well in prison. I was good at fighting, knew every curse word in the book, and was already used to eating slop. I was fully prepared to take one for the team. Unfortunately, the only effect the Visine had on my father was giving him the shits all night.

After this attempt, my resolve to kill my father remained strong. I tried various techniques ranging in efficacy from switching the pills in all his prescription bottles so he would overdose, to hiding all his socks under the mattress on his side of my parents bed to fuck with his back. I mean, I was a small child, after all, and didn't realize it actually takes quite a lot to kill another human being. Whenever I felt discouraged, I would empty bottles of Visine into my father's bottles of brown liquor. I knew at that point it wouldn't kill him, but the results were still ideal.

After my father's type-two diabetes diagnosis, I threw his last dose of insulin away, hoping it would be the final nail in the coffin for him. I still feel bad about that one to this day, not because of how it fucked him up but because my mother got a black eye for that stunt and I never owned up to it. After that murder plot, I ended the campaign against my father's life. I didn't go back to praying, though.

I mostly stopped believing in God after that and decided that if people like my father had the keys to the kingdom, I'd rather go to Hell and kick it with the likes of Elvis and Tupac. All the archangels in Heaven couldn't have changed my mind on that one. I tried to get in touch with Satan. I told him I was ready to make a deal. If he took my father out of the picture and made me a famous figure skater, he could in return have my soul. Neither of which happened, so I am assuming my soul is still intact.

In the second grade, I continued to have dreams of my father climbing into my bed late at night. One day at school, I excused myself from class to use the restroom. While dropping a deuce, I realized something was kind of stuck halfway in and halfway out, some might say prairie-doggin' it. I reached behind me to pull it out and proceed to pull what I thought was a long piece of stretchy tape out of my anus. I do remember thinking it was strange and my ass was unusually sore. It was strange at the time because as a second-grader, I wasn't in the habit of eating tape. It took me until I was an adult to realize that it was, in fact, a condom that I pulled out. To this day, I have no recollection of how it got there.

After my father spent a night in jail and lost his job due to the jobsite assault, he fell off the Jesus wagon yet again. My mother, however, still tried to keep us going to church. She found a quaint little Baptist church not far from the trailer park and proceeded to take us there every Sunday and to their youth group on Wednesdays. One Wednesday evening, we were getting ready to leave for youth group. My father was wasted from drinking all day and was feeling particularly vile. He asked my mother where the fuck she thought she was going without his permission. She told him we were going to church and she'd be back home as soon as she dropped us off. He told her she did not get to tell him where she was going; she needed to ask for permission. This was one of the few times I saw my mother stand up to my father. Thus, he proceeded to empty the contents of the kitchen cupboards onto the floor, while flinging every few dishes across the room toward my mother. "I'll fucking kill you, you cunt!" he kept screaming over and over. My mother stood there, dodging gravy dishes and wine glasses until he had run out of culinary ammunition.

"Pick this shit up!" he yelled at her and then stormed into their bedroom and slammed the door. My mother instructed all of us to get into the car and drove us to church. The entire drive there, she silently wiped tears from her eyes. When she dropped us off at the church, she told us one of the other children's mothers would be driving us home. My sister and I exchanged worried glances in the backseat, wondering if this would be the night our father would actually make good on the countless death threats he'd made against our mother over the years.

That night at youth group, the youth pastor, who was a ridiculously attractive Mexican cowboy, gave us all a tube of toothpaste, a paper plate, and a straw. He instructed us to empty the entire tube of toothpaste onto our plates. Once our tubes were empty, he told us to use the straws to try and get the toothpaste back into the tubes and if anyone managed to do it, he had a special prize for the child that could. After all the children were sufficiently frustrated from trying to achieve the impossible, he told us we could stop. He told us the toothpaste was like our words, and once we speak them we can't take them back. He told us our words matter and we should choose them with love and kindness. At this point, he gave us all ice cream sundaes and played hymns on his guitar, while his equally gorgeous wife accompanied him on vocals.

I looked down at the ice cream melting in my Styrofoam bowl with tears welling up in my eyes as I thought about all the words my father had screamed at my mother that night. The youth pastor came around the room at one point and asked me why I hadn't eaten any of my ice cream and if I was okay. I asked him what a "cunt" was. His perfectly groomed brows furrowed, and he pulled up a chair next to me, folding his hands neatly on his lap.

"Well, A. J., it's a really mean word that we shouldn't use. Did someone call you that?"

I shook my head and despite my best efforts, a couple tears spilled out onto my bowl. He put his hand on my shoulder and asked me where I had heard that word. I just shook my head and told him I didn't want to talk about it. He asked me if he could pray with me and I said, "No, thank you."

"Well, how about this, kiddo? Tonight I will pray *for* you." I wanted to tell him it wouldn't be any use. I had tried praying endlessly to no avail. But he was a pastor, after all. Maybe God listened to hot pastors' prayers more than he did little girls'. So I kept my mouth shut. His wife came over a few minutes later with an unmelted sundae for me with extra cherries and I polished it off. When we got home that night, my father had not, in fact, murdered my mother. He was passed-out drunk in bed and my mother had managed to clean up all the broken glass off the floor while we had been at church.

My father started coming to church with us again a short while after this incident, but then we left abruptly due to some incident that involved one of the deacons and my father. I was never told what transpired. But according to my father, it was because everyone who went to that church was a "fucking hypocrite." We started going to another church that was about thirty minutes away from our house after that, where my father became the youth pastor. Yep, the fucking youth pastor, guys. It would be a couple years before we stopped attending that church as well due to another "incident," and while I was never made aware of the specifics I could make a pretty confident guess that it had something to do with my father's short temper and affinity for brown liquor.

Around Y2K, my father became convinced that we were living in the end times and that Jesus was going to return and collect us, his devout followers, and take us to Heaven. The prospect of this impending rapture honestly scared the daylights out of us children. My father proceeded to have us watch Christian films about the end times and the rapture. One particular film we watched scarred me for life. It was about a group of friends who got left behind and one of them got the mark of the beast on her hand, and then she was swallowed up by the unforgiving flames of Hell. For years after this, I slept with my hands under my pillow every night so no one could come in while I was sleeping and give me the mark of the beast. If I was going to go to Hell, it was going to be on my own terms.

I have never had a party quite like that of New Year's Eve 1999. We stayed up until midnight that night and made our peace with God. I was thoroughly convinced that at the stroke of midnight my family would zap straight into the arms of Jesus and I would be left behind with nothing but piles of their clothing and the cans of food my father had been stockpiling in the pantry in anticipation of Y2K. 12:01 A.M. on New Years Day 2000 brought sweet relief when the power stayed on and our computer didn't blow up.

Chapter 3

Drug Deals and Dead Babies

Our dilapidated mobile home seemed to deteriorate more and more with each passing year. As my father became less and less employed, my mother found herself working more and more hours for minimum wage in various childcare facilities around town. As my mother's days got longer, the piles of laundry lining the hallway of our trailer grew taller. In addition to being greeted by a drunk father every day when we got home from school, we were now also greeted by the putrid odor of decay as dirty dishes piled high in the kitchen sink.

After several weeks of escalating squalor, my father decided that my sister and I were to handle the housework exclusively. We were responsible for cooking, washing dishes, cleaning, and caring for our younger sibling. My mother spent her Saturday off showing my sister and me the basics of domestic engineering. There was a steep learning curve, though, as my sister and I were seven and six, respectively, when our housekeeping shifts began.

Before we had fully mastered the art of cleaning up after a drunk sack of shit, my sister had started a load of my father's wifebeater tanks and tighty-whities in the washer. My sister had been in charge of starting the wash, as she was taller and I was an "imbecile" who couldn't tell my face hole from my asshole, according to my father. As I walked by the washer that afternoon, I threw in a red shirt my grandparents had just sent me, wanting it to be clean for school the next day. You can probably guess how those whites were going to come out. To my sister's horror, the colors bled together during the wash cycle, and my father's undergarments came out of the dryer as pink as her Barbie's stilettos. My father was enraged when he saw the clean, freshly dyed clothes that my sister had left neatly folded on his bed. He marched down the hall to our shared bedroom.

She was already nervously pacing back and forth across our room, while I sat on the floor, crisscross applesauce, innocently mining for gold in my tiny freckled nose as I played with my coveted stuffed Barney. My father threw the door open and marched inside. He had a pair of kitchen scissors in one hand, and his pink undergarments in the other.

"Anyone care to explain what the fuck this is?" he asked, holding up the pink underwear.

"I don't know what happened, Daddy!" my sister squealed. "I only ever wash the whites with whites. Mommy showed me. I didn't do anything wrong!"

My father turned to me, red-faced. "And you, A. J.? Did you put anything in the washer?"

I gulped. I knew I hadn't personally painted my father's underwear pink, but I *had* put the shirt from my grandparents in the wash. I wasn't sure how it was my fault but I knew deep down inside it was. It usually was.

"I only put one of my shirts in. I need it for school tomorrow," I said, growing more uneasy by the second.

My father's face started to turn a shade of reddish-purple. His jaw clenched so hard, the entire lower half of his face started trembling uncontrollably. He punched the wall beside him, leaving a small hole in the aftermath of his blow.

"You're gonna learn a lesson today, eh. You ruin my fucking shit and I'm gonna ruin yours."

He proceeded to rip my stuffed Barney out of my hands and decapitate him with the kitchen scissors. I screamed in horror and started sobbing as he threw the two pieces back onto my lap. He threw his underwear at my sister and hurled the scissors at the wall behind me before storming out the room. I cradled the carnage of what was left of my most prized possession as my tears fell onto his pudgy, purple body. My father yelled down the hall, summoning my sister to make him a sandwich.

"Don't worry, A. J, I'll fix it," she said to me before scurrying down the hall.

That night before bed, I got out of the bath to find my Barney carefully placed on the mattress in the corner of our room that served as my bed. My sister had used duct tape to put Barney's head back on. I looked over at her reading a Nancy Drew novel on her own mattress.

"Thanks," I said.

"You're welcome. Just hide it from Daddy for a while. He might get mad and throw it away. You need to be more careful, okay, A. J.?"

"Okay," I said.

I never touched the washing machine after that day.

Mornings during this time of my life consisted of waking up at seven to my 101 Dalmatians alarm clock, getting dressed, pouring my father a glass of whiskey, making him a toasted Spam-and-ketchup sandwich for breakfast, and racing down our half-mile drive to catch the bus with my siblings. After school, we would come home to clean up my father's lunch dishes and throw away his empty beer cans from the day. I would fold the laundry while my sister started dinner before my mother returned home, exhausted from a day spent supporting her family. After our evening chores, we would do our homework and go to bed. My sister and I both slept on mattresses situated directly on the floor. The mattresses had seen better days, as my father had rescued them from the trailer park dumpsters. They had been out in the elements for several days before my father decided that they would make an appropriate substitute for the sleeping bags we had been slumbering in on the bare floor. Dumpster mattresses were a questionable step up from the floor.

I learned how to set a mousetrap at age six. We had developed a rodent problem at the trailer and just like that, my sister and I were promoted from housewives to exterminators. My sister was responsible for disposing of the bodies when we caught them and keeping a tally of how many were killed, reporting the body count to my father. My first day of setting traps in the kitchen, I accidentally set one off on my hand. I screamed as my father laughed hysterically from the living room while my sister helped me get the trap off of my swollen red hand. She calmly reiterated the importance of proper safety protocols around a live trap, and gently iced my bruised fingers.

That night in bed, I was imagining setting a trap large enough to snap my father's neck like one of the mice my sister had walked to the dumpsters earlier that day. I thought it would be prudent to use a glass of whiskey to bait him instead of cheese. I wondered if his two front teeth would protrude as much as the mouse's from the force of the impact of the trap crushing his body. I smiled to myself, imagining the two of us dragging his body, clad in pink tighty-whities, to the dumpster like one of the mice. All of a sudden, I felt one of the creatures we were after crawl out from the inside of my mattress, scurrying over the middle of my stomach before making its way out of our bedroom and down the hall. I shuddered, cursed my father, and held my battle-scarred Barney close before eventually dozing off.

My mother was in the throes of gainful employment one fall, when a particularly nasty winter set in. Instead of making us walk the half-mile in the cold, my mother started giving one of the other mothers in the trailer park a couple bucks a week to pick us up at the bus stop with her children and drive us home. Her name was Maria and she was a tall, robust Mexican woman who wore makeup, like, a lot of makeup. My mother never wore makeup, so naturally I found the stuff fascinating.

Maria penciled on long, thin, slightly blueish eyebrows daily. Her look was not complete without heavy eyeliner and foundation that was about two shades too orange for her complexion. She wore her long, wavy black hair down and scrunched with so much gel in the morning that by evening it was so crunchy and solid, it could have probably withstood even one of my father's strongest right hooks.

Maria was a stay-at-home mom. She had a great love of floral muumuus and Jennifer Lopez. Her husband was employed as a construction worker and worked long hours outside their home. Sometimes he would take jobs out of state and be gone for weeks. Maria loved to talk about cooking and *Days of Our Lives*. I used to take notes on her recipes in my English notebook as she'd drive us home, hoping that my sister would be able to replicate them. I wish I still had them, because that woman made some dope-ass enchiladas.

One of their four children was a girl my age named Gabriela. She and I became fast friends once her mother starting picking us up from the bus stop as well. We would load up in the back of Maria's van and talk all the way back to our trailer, giggling as we sang along to Ja Rule in perfect unison. One day, I asked Gabriela about how her dad got a job working so far away from their house. I really thought it would be ideal if my father also got a job where he was gone for three weeks every couple months. She told me it was because her father was an illegal alien and had to take a lot of jobs for cash under the table. She made me pinky-promise not to tell anyone about her dad's immigration status. It was the first time in my life I had a friend tell me a secret. I told her my father was an illegal alien as well. Thus, we spent the rest of the school year making up a secret handshake and my heart was hers. And while I really wanted to know from under which table all her father's cash was magically coming, I was much more excited to finally have a best friend.

We played together most days after school and on weekends after I finished my chores. Maria's brother and sister-in-law moved into the trailer next to them that summer. On the Fourth of July that year, Maria's family hosted a BBQ and fireworks for the trailer park. I saw Gabriela's uncle up close for the first time at the celebration. His name was Antonio and he had huge muscles and tattoos that seemed to cover every inch of his body, including a couple of teardrops at the corners of his eyes. When he handed me a slice of watermelon at one point in the evening, I noticed he had the longest pinky nails I had ever seen, even longer than my mother's. I thanked him for the watermelon and scanned the crowd in search of my bestie.

"Gabby! Why is your uncle so sad? And why does he have ladies' pinky nails?" I asked her.

"He's not sad," she said, slurping down her own slice of watermelon.

"Then why did he get teardrop tattoos? It looks like he's always crying," I argued.

"Oh. Well, my mom said he got his tattoos when he was in prison. He just got out. He's a coke dealer. And I guess they need to have long nails," she responded nonchalantly.

"What's a coke dealer? Does he work for Coca-Cola? Oh my God! Do you get free soda?" I asked.

Gabriela laughed. "No, A. J. I wish I got free soda. My mom said he sells drugs and he's probably going to end up back in prison."

"Oh," I said, disappointed that the only thing Gabby and I would be sharing was a secret handshake and not a lifetime supply of my favorite soda.

Apparently, my father had bought some of Antonio's drugs that night. My father was furious for the next week, as he had said Antonio had "ripped him off" and given him something called baby laxatives. After the drug deal gone awry, I wasn't allowed to hang out with Gabriela anymore and Maria stopped picking us up from the bus stop that fall.

A few months after the drug deal, we were awoken one morning to the sound of sirens. I jumped up in my bed, assuming the police had finally come to take my father away to prison. I was hoping his life in prison would be so sad that he too would be forced to get teardrop tattoos on his face. Maybe he would become a coke dealer when he got out of prison and finally start making some money, like Gabriela's uncle. I looked out my bedroom window and saw two police cars pulling into the driveway of the trailer across the street from ours, where an ambulance and firetruck were already parked. I was so confused. The only time the police visited our neighborhood, it was to stop at our house.

The trailer across the street from us had been occupied for the last year by a young married couple who had just had a baby. They seemed nice enough and I had never heard the sound of muffled screams and breaking glass coming out of their trailer, unlike my own.

I made my way to the kitchen in my Little Mermaid pajamas, clutching my duct-taped Barney stuffy.

"What's going on across the street?" I asked my mother, who was watching everything go down from the kitchen window.

"I don't know," my mother said.

The emergency vehicles remained there for quite some time, and my parents started to lose interest in what was happening across the street and gain interest in why my sister and I thought we didn't have to start our weekend morning chores. My sister started on the laundry and dishes, and I began to take the trash out. The dumpsters in the trailer park were located right next to the trailer where all the excitement was that day. I started to cross the street to the dumpsters.

Right after I heaved the bag of waste into one of the dumpsters, I noticed two police officers exiting the front door of the trailer. A firefighter behind them carried something small wrapped in a white blanket out to the ambulance. Following behind the firefighter was the young couple who lived there. The husband was holding firmly to the upper body of his wife, who came out of the trailer screaming, thrashing like a wild animal in his arms, her arms outstretched behind the back of the firefighter. She was clawing at the air frantically as if she was drowning in it.

I had heard my parents scream at the top of their lungs on many occasions, but the sounds coming out of this woman were unlike anything I had ever heard. She clawed at her husband's hands, desperately trying to free herself, as she screamed behind the firefighter.

"My baby! My baby!" she howled over and over again. The firefighter gently handed the tiny bundle over to a paramedic, who proceeded to load it into the back of the ambulance; he turned to the woman, trying to console her. Her husband finally lost his hold on her and she fell to her knees in her driveway and screamed, holding her face in her hands. The noises coming out her body sounded like a demon was trying to crawl his way out of her throat and swallow up the whole trailer park in one gulp. I ran back across the street as fast as my little feet would carry me and back into our trailer. It was the only time in my life I wanted to flee into that trailer and not from it. But I would have done anything to escape the sound of that woman's screams that day. I wasn't praying much by that point, but that night I said a prayer for the woman and her baby.

I would find out later that her baby had pulled a blanket that was on the side of the crib down on his face and suffocated on it that night while everyone was sleeping. The mother had come into the nursery to get her baby up in the morning and found him dead. The couple moved out a few short months after their baby died and all the children in the trailer park became convinced that their trailer was haunted by the baby's ghost. Little did they know that the real monster in our ramshackle neighborhood was a living human being I happened to call Dad.

Chapter 4

Murder in the Desert

My grandparents essentially funded my childhood. When the cupboards were bare, my father would make my mother get on the phone and call her parents to ask for money. My mother and I would drive forty-five minutes to the nearest Western Union, which was located inside a Safeway, to collect the wire transfer because, my friends, this was the 90s. There was no Venmo, no Cash App. We loaded our asses into our God-awful baby-blue station wagon that we called "The Shitmobile" and we drove to get that paper. My mother would always take me to the Starbucks inside the Safeway and let me get a tall Vanilla Frappuccino. Western Union days were the best. Because of my grandparents' generosity, we were able to take a lot of road trips out to California to see them. Road trips were kind of like "Mr. Toad's Wild Ride" in my family, as my father had a great love of driving us cross-country wasted. All the shit seemed to really go down on the journey home for some reason.

On one particular journey, somewhere in Utah my father pulled into a gas station to fill up. We had been driving for hours and we all had to use the restroom. As all the kids piled out of the backseat of our car, I was the last to jump out. On my exit, my hand somehow got sliced by the exposed gears on the side of the door. The cut was so deep in my pinky, I could see everything from my tendons down to the little white bone in the middle of my finger. I looked down at my throbbing finger and let out a blood-curdling scream. My mother rushed over to me and also starting screaming when she saw my finger. My father came over and said through clenched teeth as he peered nervously over his shoulder, "Calm down. Calm the fuck down, Deb!"

"We need to call 911, Greg. Her finger's almost ripped off!" my mother shrieked. At this point, several onlookers had started to notice the commotion coming from our pump.

A frail older couple approached us. "Oh, dear," the woman said, "that does look nasty, doesn't it? I'll go inside and call the hospital." She wrapped her arm around my shoulders and gave me a comforting squeeze.

"She'll be fine. We're are going to drive her there right now," my father said as he jerked my shoulder away from the older woman.

He grabbed some paper towels from the window-washing station beside the pump and hastily wrapped them around my wounded appendage. The older woman looked at me apprehensively and eventually nodded her head and made her way back to her own pump. We all loaded into the car and my father peeled out of the gas station and back onto the highway.

"Where is the nearest hospital?" my mother asked as we raced down the road.

"We're not taking her to the hospital, Deb, you fucking idiot. Do you know how much that will cost? Do you want them to take our kids away? We are stopping at the next gas station and getting some butterfly bandages and gauze, and she'll be fucking fine."

The silent sobs I had been trying to stifle in the backseat had at this point started to become audible.

My father whipped his head around and stuck his pudgy finger in my face. "Stop crying, you little shit. If you weren't so fucking careless, this never would have happened."

"Greg!" my mother interjected.

"Oh, shut the fuck up, Deb. I'll leave you here. Right here in the fucking desert, and you'll never see your kids again, you hear me? Everybody shut the fuck up!"

I looked down at my hand covered in paper towels. They were soaked in blood that had started to drip onto the seat of the car I was occupying. As my hand started trembling uncontrollably, I looked away from my hand and around the car, trying to stifle a sudden wave of nausea. I figured I might manage to survive my father's wrath for injuring my finger, but *surely* he would murder me if I puked in the car.

We did, in fact, stop at the next gas station and my father gruffly dressed my wound in the parking lot, where he proceeded to dump rubbing alcohol on my wound and close it with bandages. I bit down on the inside of cheek until I tasted blood as the alcohol hit the carnage that was left of my finger, resisting the urge to scream. My mother spent the new few weeks changing the dressings daily. My mangled finger eventually closed. It wasn't pretty, though. I lost all feeling in the middle of my right pinky and got a nasty scar that extends almost the whole length of the finger. To this day, I have permanent nerve damage in that finger.

My father actually did end up leaving my mother in the desert a few years later. We were headed back from another trip visit my grandparents. That trip was particularly painful, as we had only brought one CD for the whole trip and it was a collection of the 1998 Grammy Nominees. My grandparents had funded a rental car for our family, as none of our vehicles were reliable enough to make the journey. It was quite exciting to be in a car fancy enough to be equipped with a CD player, but the initial thrill quickly wore off as fifteen hours of Hansen and Shania Twain would make anyone homicidal. So needless to say, the energy was tense.

My father had started drinking somewhere in Nevada and began to black out in Arizona. We knew he was drunk, because he started playing "Where Have All the Cowboys Gone?" by Paula Cole on an endless loop. We eventually fell asleep and were awoken a while later by my father's screams.

"Where's your mom? Where's your fucking mom?" he screamed.

Startled, I started frantically looking around the car for our mother, as we were doing about 90 down the highway in the wee hours of the morning. I initially thought it must be some sort of trick question. Like, was this my father's sick version of "I Spy"? Was my mother going to suddenly pop out of the dash? If we answered incorrectly, would we get hit? I carefully thought about what the safest answer would be. I finally settled on "I don't know."

"She's fucking dead. Kids, your mom is dead." He pulled over onto the side of the highway and put both his hands on his head as he started to hyperventilate. "She's dead. She must have fallen out of the car. We need to go to the police."

He ripped back onto the highway and drove on until we found a small police station in the next town. My sister had been quietly crying into her hands, while I had been spending the drive contemplating also jumping out of the car. Better dead than stuck with this fat fuck, I thought to myself.

We scurried into the police station behind my father. Once inside, my father slammed his arms repeatedly onto the front desk in a Mussolini-esque fashion. "I need to report my wife missing! We need to call the FBI!" The man who was working the front desk had been enjoying a cigarette as we walked in. His stringy blond hair was cut into a perfect mullet with a handlebar mustache to boot.

He stood up as he put out the cigarette he had been smoking in an ashtray sitting next to him. "Okay, sir, why don't y'all come with me?"

We followed the mullet back to an interrogation room, where my father proceeded to tell him about how my mother mysteriously fell out of the car somewhere between Nevada and Arizona but he didn't know where and he couldn't remember what happened.

"Okay, sir. Now, have you had anything to drink this evening?"

"I don't drink," my father said. "I'm just tired. We had a long trip and I'm just trying to get my family home safe. Oh, Debbie!" he cried. "Not my Debbie!"

I don't know why my father's acting career never took off, because I really thought he deserved an Oscar for that fucking performance.

The officer scribbled a few notes on a small notepad and then stood up quite suddenly. "Well, I think I've got everything I need for right now. I just need to have you fill out some paperwork. How 'bout you kiddos wait here for your daddy to fill out this paperwork, and we'll get you some sodas while you wait?"

My father followed the officer out of the room. We were there for a few minutes when another officer not dressed in uniform but instead a rather snazzy suit came in without my father. My sister and I exchanged worried glances as we squeezed closer together on the chair we were sharing.

"Hey, kids, my name is Officer Yoder, and I would like to ask you a couple questions. Would that be okay?"

"Where's our daddy?" my sister asked nervously.

"Oh, he's finishing up his paperwork up front. These kinds of things take a lot of paperwork, so he might be up there a while. But I'll tell you what, I won't tell him anything you tell me. You won't get in trouble for talking to the police. We are here to help, okay?"

My sister and I nodded in unison.

"Now, do you two know where your mama is?" the officer asked.

"No, we were all asleep," my sister said.

"Well, our dad said our mom is dead," I said.

My sister jabbed her elbow deep into my side.

"What? He did!" I said indignantly.

The officer started scribbling furiously in his notebook. "Did your daddy hurt your mommy?" he asked.

My sister's head sunk and she whimpered, "I don't know."

The officer put his hand on her knee and got a little closer to us. In a lowered voice, he said, "It's okay. You can tell me. Did you see your daddy hurt your mommy?"

My sister started to cry so hard, she couldn't seem to form any words.

"We were sleeping. We didn't see anything. Is our mom dead?" I asked the officer.

"Well, let's not get ahead of ourselves here, kids. How about I go get those sodas we promised you?"

He walked out of the room and a woman came in with two grape sodas for us. After she left, it felt like we were alone in that room for hours. Eventually they brought our father back into the room and let him use the phone to call my grandparents to inform them that my mother was missing. My grandfather answered the phone. As soon as my father told him that my mother was missing, an explosion of muffled expletives started to erupt from the receiver. My father kept telling my grandfather to calm down and tried to get him to repeat something he had said. I couldn't make out much since the call wasn't on speaker, but I'm pretty sure I made out the phrase "you fucking idiot" a few times. My father ended up hanging up on my grandfather as he continued to curse him from the other end of the line.

"Thank God. Your mother is okay. She's at a truck stop a couple hundred miles from here. We must have forgotten her. We're all just so tired. Thank you so much for your help, Officers. Oh, thank you, Jesus. My Debbie's okay! Sorry to have wasted your time."

And a short while later, we were backtracking back to the truck stop, where my mother had used a pay phone to call her parents and let them know she was stranded.

You see, what happened was, my father was so blacked out that when my mother had come back to the car from the truck stop, she had put something in the trunk. When she slammed the trunk door, my father must have thought it was her getting in the car so he peeled out of the parking lot, not noticing her frantically screaming and running behind him. He kept driving through the blackout until he came to and realized my mother wasn't in the car.

The entire drive back to the truck stop, my father was eerily quiet. When we finally arrived at the truck stop, my mother was sitting on a bench outside. She jerked up as she saw the car pull in. She ran over to us and opened the passenger door. "Oh my God, I was so worried! Thank God you're back! Greg, I need four bucks. I had to eat so I got a burger inside and told them I would pay them as soon as you got here."

"Get in the car, Deb," my father said.

"But Greg, I need to pay them. They gave me food."

My father's jaw clenched and a vein in his forehead started to throb as he said in a voice so low and slow it made the hair on my arms stand at full attention, "I said, get in the car, Deb."

My mother looked back wearily at the truck stop and then got in the front seat. My father put his hand gently on the back of my mother's head and in an instant slammed her head onto the front dash.

"You stupid fucking bitch! You know how much gas we wasted because of you? Stupid fucking cunt. I should have just left you here."

My mother cried into the napkin she was using to sop up her freshly bloodied nose. And with that, we were back on the road again.

Our trips to California to visit my grandparents were the highlight of my childhood. I loved California. The palm trees, the ocean, Disneyland, and my grandparents' house; it was Heaven on Earth. My grandparents were saints, and did their best to give us a great childhood from afar. Whenever we would visit, they would take us to Disneyland and Universal Studios. My favorite ride at Disneyland was and still is The Haunted Mansion. From a young age, I saw an incredible beauty in all things dark and twisty. I think in some strange way, it made me believe there was hope for girls like me. I was never the pretty princess in the fairytales, sucking on a silver spoon from birth and shitting unicorns and rainbows. I was more like the troll under the bridge that reeked of piss and poverty.

On one of our Universal Studios visits, my father was pretty deep down some conspiracy theory rabbit holes. During that trip, my siblings and I were obsessed with the ET ride. As you got to the front of the line, an attendant sitting behind a computer asked for your name and printed out a card that you used to get on the ride. My father pulled us aside and told us it was the government trying to get our identities with our fingerprints on the cards, so we were instructed to give the attendant a fake name. When my turn came, I told the attendant my name was Britney Spears. She stopped typing and looked up from her computer, pulling her glasses down the bridge of her nose.

"Yeah, okay, honey." She handed me my freshly printed card that read "Britney Spears," and I was convinced she actually believed that I was, in fact, Britney Spears in disguise just trying to enjoy the ET ride at Universal Studios without having to sign autographs all day. I reluctantly handed what I was sure was my ticket to fame to the next attendant and boarded my bicycle.

Chapter 5

Black Coffee and Baby Boomers

My grandparents were a beacon of light throughout my childhood. My great-grandmother's son, my grandpa, was the only solid male role model I had growing up. And although we didn't get to see them as often as I would have liked, I greatly cherished the time we did have. My mother's parents were originally from the Black Hills of South Dakota, but in 1962 they took his motorcycle out to Southern California and never looked back.

My grandpa was a bad-ass motherfucker. He rode a motorcycle and worked as a metrologist calibrating specialty scales. One time his work even sent him to Egypt to fix something. So naturally, I thought he was a spy. There was nowhere he went without his cowboy boots and tobacco pipe. There was nothing he couldn't fix, expect perhaps for my mother's choice in men.

He was a man of few words. They were usually curse words when he was out tinkering in his garage on various projects. And while by all outside appearances he seemed pretty rough around the edges, he was, in fact, a softie. I followed that man everywhere, worshipping the ground he walked on every step of the way. He would hand me his toolbox and say, "Well, babe, let's go fix some shit." And I would carry it following close on his heels, my tiny frame wobbling from the weight of all his tools. He probably spent most of his life in the garage, but to me he was the most interesting man in the world.

He had made up code names for all the tools. A Phillips screwdriver was a "dinglehopper" and the flathead a "doodlebug." I would sit next to him in silence for hours as he tinkered. "A. J., I need the dinglehopper," he would say with his hand outstretched. I would pop up in an instant and grab him the tool he required. My first serious boyfriend thought I was insane when I asked him once where the dinglehopper was so I could fix a loose cupboard in his apartment.

Whenever he was in the garage, he would have a can of Miller High Life in one hand and a tool in the other. I recall wondering what it would take to convince my father to switch to drinking High Life. I figured if my grandpa could have six of them and still be an angel, it might do the same for my father. And according to my grandpa, it was the champagne of beers, which sounded kind of fancy.

Over the course of my childhood, my grandpa picked up where his mother left off, teaching me how to do life. He always drove a red Pontiac Fiero when I was growing up. Whenever he and my grandma would take road trips out to visit us in Colorado, he would take me on long drives. We would listen to Creedence Clearwater Revival and Van Morrison the whole time. He would look over at me every time "Brown-Eyed Girl" came on. "You're my green-eyed girl," he would sing over to me. I rolled my window down and let my hand ride with the wind. I wished those rides would last forever. I would squeal with delight as he'd pull into empty parking lots and rip donuts. "Donuts, Grandpa. Donuts!!!" I would beg him every morning he'd wake up at our trailer.

"Gotta have my fuel first, babe," he would say as he drank his decaf coffee and dipped his toast in the bacon grease. One morning, he let me try his coffee, as I was relentless in my efforts to emulate everything he did. "That'll put some hair on your chest, kid," he said, handing me the cup of black coffee. I choked it down, forcing a smile. "Mmm, delicious," I said, secretly wanting to vomit. Today, I take my coffee black and my toast dipped in bacon grease.

When I was eleven, my grandpa went from being the one who ripped the donuts to teaching me how to rip them. I learned how to drive a stick at eleven because of him. He also taught me how to change a tire and check my oil.

My grandpa was an avid fisherman. Every year, he took a week-long fishing trip on the Colorado River with his brother. Sometimes when he would visit us, he would take me fishing. He taught me how to bait a line and gut a fish in thirty seconds. Initially, I lacked the patience and steadfastness required to have any measure of success at fishing. After a few years, though, I got pretty good and we started to have contests for who would catch the most fish while we were out.

"Pretty close, babe," he would say as I held up my two fish next to his string of eight.

Every trip, my grandpa made it a point to set aside one morning where he would take me to a diner for a breakfast date, just the two of us. I would be so proud walking into those restaurants with him hand in hand, just me and my grandpa. We would both order decaf coffees, black. I got a lot of weird looks from servers as they would hand me my coffee, at least until I became a teenager. I'm sure it was kind of weird bringing out a piping-hot mug of black coffee and setting it in front of a six-year-old. We would talk about music and cars, giggling over our eggs as we joked about who would catch the biggest fish on our next trip to the lake. He would talk about the basics of engine repair and how it was important to learn how to do things for myself and not depend on anyone else. At the end of our meals, I would thank him. "What? Did you think I was gonna take you to some dive?" he would always ask me with a wink.

My grandma was the yin to my grandpa's yang. Where he was a grumpy old curmudgeon, she was a sweet little old lady. She was a retired kindergarten teacher who loved sunflowers and Coca-Cola. According to Greg, she was a "flaming liberal," as her beloved cat was named Mikhail Gorbachev, whom we all called Gorby for short. My father was very adamant that the only thing worse in this world than a lesbian was a liberal. So naturally, I decided that when I grew up I would be both.

My grandmother was not a drinker, but she always told me that Coca-Cola was her only vice. Apparently she had an allergy to something in them, and they would burn like fire down her throat. But she had one every day. Every morning when she was in town, she would sit at the kitchen table with her coffee and a stack of postcards, writing in her perfect penmanship about her adventures to whoever was on the receiving end. I used to wonder if she sent postcards to everyone in the world. We would walk them to the mailboxes together to send them off. She would take long, deep breaths, taking in the scenery around her.

"Isn't this lovely, A. J.?" she would say, looking around. I always thought the trailer park was kind of a shit hole, but I went along with it. My grandma could see the beauty in anything.

She was a big fan of literature and kindness. Every trip, she would take us kids shopping for books and clothes for the coming school year.

My grandma also had an affinity for gel pens and journals. She in turn instilled in me a great love of office supplies and journaling. To this day, I have a vast collection of worn-out journals I've spent my life filling front to back, because as my grandma taught me, once you start something you finish it. An ex-boyfriend also taught me to be more careful where I leave them out. So if you're reading this, Steve, go fuck yourself. But thank you for that valuable life lesson.

My grandparents' visits were a sweet slice of Heaven for me. Whenever they were in town, the cupboards were full and my father was always on his best behavior. They would take us to do all manner of fun things. My grandma would take us to any museum she could find and I developed a great love of history and museums because of her. I was thoroughly convinced that if anyone could figure out how to build a time machine, it would be my grandpa. I was sure that one day, he would take me back in a time to meet my hero, the "Unsinkable" Molly Brown, in person.

When their trips inevitably came to an end, I was always gutted. We would all gather in the driveway exchanging hugs and farewells. As we watched them pull out of driveway we wiped our tears, knowing that life would now return to normal. The only dry eyes in the crowd were my father's. He would head back inside and pour himself a large glass of whiskey, relishing that he was now reinstated as the man of the house, king of the roach motel.

Chapter 6

Rocket Man

A true conman, my father was always scheming. Looking back, I do wonder if he had applied himself to gainful employment and citizenship with the same fervor that he did his various schemes, if we would have been millionaires.

When he was working, money was tight. When he wasn't working, money was something we kind of thought was real, but couldn't be quite sure, like the Land of Narnia. Because the trailer park we lived in was located in such a rural area, a lot of driving was required to get us anywhere we needed to go. When we didn't have enough money for gas, my father would siphon it from various locations. When I was little, he would pack my sister and me in the backseat of the station wagon late at night while my mother was sleeping and take us to car garages and auto-body shops. He would park the car next to our target vehicle, grab the clear plastic-straw tube he used to draw the gas, and have my sister and me keep a lookout while he did the deed.

While working on construction jobsites, he learned that copper had a good amount of value. He would work during the day, taking note of the various copper-wire caches around the jobsite. At night, my sister and I would return with him to collect the goods. We would run around the site, seeing who could procure the most bronze pirate's booty, giggling the entire time. That shit was like Treasure Island. He would drive us around town on the weekends, drinking a 40 and feeling out his various contacts to find one who was willing to buy the copper. If he sold copper that day, we would get milkshakes. The copper scheme was my personal favorite.

Being a has-been actor, my father had an intense passion for cinema. We couldn't afford to buy movies, so my father's fucked-up wheels started turning. There was a small corner store in our town that had a rental movie section. It was limited, for sure, but they did have a few bangers in stock. My mother would take us to the store with a list of the films my father wanted. We would rent the films on my parents' account and take them home. If we found all the films on the list, we would spend the weekend watching all of them, while my father pirated them onto another VHS machine. He would meticulously put a long rectangular sticker onto the tape and write the name of the film on the sticker. And thus, our film collection grew. If we couldn't find all the films on the list, my mother usually got a black eye and we hid in our rooms until the dust had settled.

My parents, however, neglected to pay the charges on their ever-growing charge account at the corner store. I witnessed a particularly awkward interaction between my mother and the woman who owned the corner store with her husband one day.

"Look, Deb. I can't give you any more shit. Your account is $220 in the red and you've given me two bad checks. I'm not taking another check and you guys can't buy anything here until you're all paid up," she said. Her name was Rhonda. She had long, fiery-red curly hair and the voice of a man from smoking two packs of Pall Malls a day.

"Please, Rhonda. Just let me get this and then I'll make it right," my mother said, anxiously looking down at the VHS tapes, salt-and-vinegar chips, and Diet Pepsis she had laid out on the counter.

"No, honey. I'm sorry, but I'm puttin' my foot down today. I mean, you guys don't even rewind the tapes, for Christ's sake!" Rhonda said, folding her arms behind the counter.

We left the corner store that day emptyhanded. I was sweating bullets on my mother's behalf the whole way home. I mean, I saw the way my father reacted when we couldn't bring *Field of Dreams* home one day. I feared that to our father, our failed corner store trip would go down in history as the worst attempted invasion of all time, including Operation Barbarossa. This was the Operation Barbarossa of pirated VHS films.

Remarkably, when we arrived home, my father was about three Vicodin and four shots of Crown in. He was like Mother-fucking Teresa when we walked in the front door. He smiled when we came in and listened as my mother frantically explained what had happened at the corner store that day, nodding his head periodically. He chewed on her words for a moment, as we all waited with baited breath, wondering if any of us would survive the night.

"Well, I think it's time we get ourselves a Blockbuster membership, don't you think?" my father calmly said.

My mother's jaw dropped, as if someone had just walked in our front door and given her a check for a hundred thousand dollars.

And thus, we began pirating our films from the local Blockbuster. Y'all can talk as much shit as you want about Blockbuster today, but back then their selection was fire. Being still slightly traumatized from the corner store incident, my mother did her best to make sure we were kind, so we *did* always rewind before returning our videos from that point forward.

While my father was working on construction sites, he was also deep in the throes of alcoholism and a pesky little pain pill problem. He was employed as a tile layer. My father had been let go from a few jobs for his substance-abuse issues. It was then that he decided his children needed some real-world experience. He would call my sister and me out of school for a week here and there and bring us to work with him.

And so we began our education at the school of hard knocks, where we would eventually graduate summa cum laude. My father spent several days teaching us how to lay tile. My many years of tinkering with my grandfather qualified me to operate the wet saw when my father was too drunk to do so. It was actually kind of fun. My father gave us five dollars for every day of our manual labor, which seemed like a fortune at the time. On the drive home he would blast golden oldies and stop at a gas station for some Bugles and Cokes. It was one of the few times growing up that my father actually seemed to enjoy having us around.

At one particularly snazzy jobsite, my father pilfered some leftover black marble tile. That weekend, he instructed that my sister and I lay the tile in the "master bath" of our trailer. I was so proud of the job we did. My father took us to the Dairy Queen after we finished to acknowledge a job well done. I loved laying tile. And it was one of the few things on the planet that seemed to make my father happy besides pain pills, so life was good. When my father got fired from that gig, I was devastated.

After he lost his job, my father had quite a few tools and nothing to do with them. It was then that he discovered the great American staple that is pawn shops. He took his tools in and pawned them from time to time when we needed money and couldn't get any from my grandparents. He would blow the money on Crown, pills, chips, and keeping our Blockbuster account in the black. Whatever was left over, my mother took to the grocery store. She usually came home with ramen packets, Spam, and potatoes.

Once my father discovered pawn shops, none of our personal belongings were safe. We lost a good many items to those shops. My younger brother's PlayStation One (yep, you heard that right, Gen Z, PLAYSTATION ONE), his Nintendo DS, my sister's silver earrings from my grandparents, and a locket from my great-grandmother were all eventually lost to pawn shops. Even my mother's wedding band wasn't safe.

Newly unemployed and still on recreational pain pills, my father found himself with a lot of spare time of his hands. Our dial-up internet had recently gotten cut off due to our delinquent account, so my father started getting creative. He went through an arts-and-crafts phase that was quite enjoyable to watch. His mother had passed from lung cancer in July of 1990, a couple weeks before I was born. I never got to meet her, but according to my father she was a saint.

He would go through phases where he missed her exceptionally hard, during which he would instill in us a great fear of smoking cigarettes and a profound respect for WWII veterans. In one of these phases, he decided the best way to honor her memory was to start crocheting just like she did. My grandparents had just sent us money for groceries, but instead of buying food my father used the money to buy an assortment of crochet hooks and yarn. I watched as he tried to replicate one of the faded blue-and-beige chevron blankets his mother had left him.

He would drink his whiskey and curse as he tried to master a double-crochet. Maybe if YouTube had existed back then, he would have seen more success. He would stitch in silence for a few minutes before cursing and unraveling all the shoddy work he had done. If he hadn't been such a prick to me all the time, I might have shown him a thing or two about how to crochet like a mother-fucker, like my great-grandmother had taught me how to when I was only four. Instead, I watched him suffer in silence, laughing to myself as he agonized over each stitch. Fucking amateur, I thought to myself.

Eventually, he would abandon his mission to master the art of crochet. Naturally, he moved on to popsicle sticks. He actually had a knack for it and I watched in awe as he meticulously assembled tiny villages of popsicle-stick houses that he would paint various colors upon completion. Each village was complete with a theme. One was an old western town that my father populated with my younger brother's tiny plastic Army men. His craftsmanship was honestly impressive. He eventually gave that up too when he became so constipated from the pain pills that he "couldn't focus on his art," as he told my mother. The popsicle-stick villages would remain in our home until my graduation from high school.

During my father's arts-and-crafts phase, he decided he was also a carpenter, probably due to his success with popsicle sticks. He randomly declared one day that my sister and I would no longer be sharing a bedroom. At the time, my younger brother had his own room and my sister and I shared one. My father moved my brother into the room with my sister, and I got my brother's room. My father built me a raised bed that had two walk-in closet areas underneath made out of plywood and two-by-fours. He constructed a ladder at the end of the bed so I could access the top, where my mattress was located.

Once my new bed was completed, I was excited to have my own room. I didn't know what I had done to deserve this honor, but I didn't question it. It was during this time that the dreams of my father coming into my room at night became more vivid and violent, and sometimes they didn't quite feel like dreams, more like a hazy state where I wasn't fully awake but wasn't fully asleep. I'd have flashes of my father slapping me and climbing on top of me, telling me not to make a sound or he would hurt me. I would awake in the morning covered in the smell of whiskey and sore in places that I didn't quite yet understand. I didn't know what was happening to me, but I started to have feelings of deep disgust every time I looked at my father. After about a year, I was moved back into the room with my sister and the dreams stopped for good.

One year for Christmas, my grandparents sent me fifty dollars. I think my father was too scared of the repercussions in the form of my grandpa to take the money from me. I decided the best way to spend my newfound wealth was to get a fish tank. I selected ten fish from the pet store and my heart was full. I named them all. Although, to this day, I only remember one fish's name. His name was Kevin. I named him Kevin Costner, as I had decided that maybe one day he would be my husband because he made me feel some type of way. I was greedy, I'll admit it. As time wore on, however, I realized that the upkeep of a fish tank was quite a lot of work. I didn't know you had to clean it regularly.

Drunk as a skunk one day, my father informed me that if I didn't start cleaning my fish tank he would walk it to the trailer park dumpsters and throw it in, fish and all. I asked him how people cleaned fish tanks. He walked out of the trailer and grabbed the siphon we used to procure our gasoline from the car trunk. When he came back inside, he threw the hose at me. At this point in my life, I had watched my father siphon so much gas, I could have replicated the process in my sleep. I expertly used the siphon to clean out the bottom of tank.

When I woke up the next morning, all the fish in my tank were belly up. I guess some gasoline was left in the siphon and poisoned my fish, including Kevin Costner. I was devastated. My father told my sister to help me carry the tank outside and dump the water and the fish outside. I cursed myself while I carried the tank out with her. When we dumped it out, I saw Kevin's lifeless body flop out onto the browned grass of our backyard. I couldn't bear to leave him there, naked and exposed.

I ran inside and grabbed a shoebox and a purple marker. I cradled Kevin's lifeless body as I put him in the shoebox. I neatly printed his name on the box as I whispered to him that I loved him in *Waterworld*. My sister used a shovel to dig a small hole and we buried Kevin, while saying a few words in his memory. When we brought the fish tank inside, we were instructed to wash it out in the kitchen sink and after it dried, my father used the glass remains to host his CD collection.

At one point, the "Shitmobile" shit the bed. Unfortunately, it happened in the parking lot of a bar that my father frequented that was about twenty miles from our home. The bar threatened to tow the car if he didn't get it out of the lot, so he made a plan to retrieve it himself. He loaded a tow rope and the lot of us into our dilapidated Bronco to retrieve the "Shitmobile" from the bar one night after closing time.

When we arrived at our destination, my father started to connect the station wagon to the Bronco with the tow cord. My mother and we children were to remain in the car behind the Bronco while he towed us. He gave my mother careful instructions as to how she was to brake when he braked and turn when he turned during the tow operation. She nodded intently as he proceeded to drink out of a handle of whiskey, checking the connection between the two vehicles.

As we were in the car behind him, things were going smooth. My mother's knuckles glared white in the moonlight as she followed behind my father, braking when he braked, turning when he turned. It's kind of ironic that shit went downhill as we were going uphill. As we were going up a rather large hill on our way back to the trailer park, the rope that was connecting the two vehicles snapped and the station wagon started rolling backwards. As my mother screamed in horror, I genuinely thought we were going to die that night. Somehow my mother managed to pull the emergency brake and skid to stop at the bottom of the hill.

Meanwhile, my father had turned the Bronco around once he realized we were no longer in tow and met us at the bottom of the hill. He ran up to the car flailing his arms wildly. My mother looked at him approaching us and took a deep breath before she scrambled to unroll the hand-crank window of the station wagon.

He grabbed her by the throat and began to cuss her out.

"You stupid cunt! You had one job. One fucking job!" he screamed.

She coughed violently as she twisted her upper body to escape his grasp. She finally managed to pull herself free, for which he rewarded her with a slap to the face. Somehow, my father managed to reconnect the broken tow rope back together and we made it home safely. My mother silently followed my father the rest of the way home, as "Rocket Man" by Elton John blared on the radio.

My sister and I started singing along but with lyrics we crafted ourselves, commemorating the events that had transpired that evening.

"We're driving along and the rope broke…. And I think we're gonna be in deep, deep shit…," we sang along. We completed the ditty with synchronized hand movements. For years we sang that song, much to the disdain of my mother.

Chapter 7

Pets and Prejudice

We only had one dog growing up. It was a chihuahua named Julio. He was tan with black paws and the most adorable little button nose I had ever seen. I was so excited to finally have a pet and thought he was the sweetest little biscuit. To this day, I don't think I've ever fallen in love with a person the way I fell in love with that dog. He unfortunately didn't feel the same. As I would squeeze him and whisper sweet nothings into his ear, he would curl his upper lip and snap at my face. Still, I persisted. I was determined to make Julio love me. I would sneakily feed him pieces of Spam and Hamburger Helper under the dinner table. He would thank me by licking my toes. I would cough, trying to hold my giggles in at the table, afraid he would blow our cover with his little licks of gratitude.

My sister and I would walk him around the trailer park, fighting over who would get to hold his leash. We reveled in the fact that the other children were jealous of the adorable creature who had come into our lives. We did have to warn them not to get to close, though, as Julio would do his best to take a chunk out of their faces if they tried to pet him. Julio seemed to enjoy our walks as well, as long as there were no children around. His adorable little curled tail would wag furiously as we passed bunnies and groundhogs on our way.

Julio had his issues, though. He couldn't seem to make it outside to drop a deuce. Instead, he would relieve himself on the shaggy brown carpet of our living room. My father would explode when he saw Julio's little presents and proceed to pick the poor dog up and throw his tiny body across the room. My sister and I had watched my father beat Julio enough that we decided it was time to intervene and shield our dog from my father's wrath.

We would grab paper towels and try to clean up all of Julio's messes before my father could see them, scrubbing the floor furiously. We were successful in this for a couple weeks until one night around bedtime, Julio soiled the living room carpet right in front of my father. My sister and I looked at each other in horror, and waited for what was sure to be the ultimate display of my father's rage.

My father chugged the rest of the glass of whiskey he had been enjoying and popped out of his chair, grabbing his car keys off of the kitchen counter.

"Well, fucker, let's go for a drive," he said to Julio before swooping him up in his arms and walking out the front door.

We never saw Julio again.

I cried in bed every night for weeks, so sad that the dog I had so desperately wanted to love me was gone forever. I hated my father for taking him away from us. I briefly tossed around the idea of resuming my assassination attempts of my father, but decided I wasn't really strong enough to kill him yet.

We never had another pet after that. From that night forward, my father said pets were "freeloaders" and made the house smell like shit. I felt the same way about him, but whatever.

My mother would sometimes bring movies home from Blockbuster for us kids. We had an extensive selection of non-pirated Disney VHS tapes from my grandparents, but other than that pickings were slim. I think my mother knew this and she would bring home various movies she thought we'd like if she managed to find all of my father's choices on the list that day. He was always in a good mood when she accomplished this, and was fairly pleasant for the weekend as we worked our way through his film selections.

One Friday afternoon, my mother brought home *The Nutty Professor*. My father snatched it off the kitchen table when he saw it.

"What the fuck is this shit, Deb?" he asked my mother.

"Oh. Well, it was one of their weekly specials. I thought the girls would like it," my mother anxiously explained, looking down at her feet.

"Deb, you fucking idiot. This is a *black* movie. Do we look black to you, hmm?" he asked.

My mother looked around nervously and started to stumble over her words.

"These aren't as good as our movies. Not that you would understand good cinema, Deb. Don't bring this shit home again," he explained as he held the tape in his hands, waving it in unison with the inflection of his words.

That was the first night I heard the "n" word. My brother was around five at this time and must have thought the word sounded silly, as he proceeded to bounce around the kitchen, saying it over and over.

"Hamilton!" my mother said to my brother.

"Oh, shut the fuck up, Deb," my father said.

My brother did end up getting in trouble for repeating it at kindergarten the following Monday. We were not allowed to watch the film, and my mother was instructed to return it the next day.

I didn't hear that word come out of my father's mouth that much. However, one year a black family moved into the trailer where the baby had died. We heard it a lot that year.

Aside from that, my father directed most of his racism at the Mexican families that lived in the trailer park and worked on jobs with him. At one point in my childhood, my father's immigration status changed from illegal alien to resident alien, after which he proceeded to talk mad shit about illegal aliens, especially Gabriela's father.

I couldn't understand how her father was different from mine. They were both working for cash under that magical table. They both came from different countries, and they both worked in construction. It was during that time that I began to understand that my father, for some reason, thought he was better than people with brown or black skin. I honestly wished that Gabriela's dad could have been mine.

He seemed like such a nice guy. When he would return from his long trips working away from home, all his children would run to him, squealing with joy. He would outstretch his arms and they would line up, taking turns as he tossed each one of them up in the air. As he caught them, he would shower them with hugs and kisses and they would all head into their trailer, giddy that their father was home once again.

I had never been happy to see my father arrive home. I could never describe the feelings I had when my father would arrive home from work until much later in life, when a doctor told me it was time to have my first colonoscopy. It was very similar to that feeling. As my father's immigration status changed and his hate for Mexicans grew, I developed a great disdain for Canadians for a while.

I didn't understand how a country could create one of the meanest men to walk the face of the earth. I do regret my hatred of Canadians and have come to understand that they are lovely people and they are actually extremely polite. Maybe they kicked my father out of their beautiful country because he was such a prick. I mean, they did produce Celine Dion, after all.

Chapter 8

Hogwarts and Boy Bands

Reading became a delightful escape for me as a child. I had a very vivid imagination, and loved any opportunity to journey into another world through a good story. I would hide away, tucked safely in the pages of other people's stories from what was happening in my own home. I was constantly being told what I could and could not do, but I found books offered me a magical portal to temporary freedom. However, my father had a very extensive list of books and music we were not permitted to experience due to their "secular" nature. One Christmas, we were in California visiting my grandparents and one of my aunts had gotten me a Spice Girls CD. My father ripped it out of my hands right after I had opened it and gave it back to my aunt, telling her we weren't allowed to listen to that garbage.

Later that evening, my aunt caught my mother and my sister and me alone in the bedroom we were staying in. She asked my mother why my father was so controlling. After all, it was just pop music. There weren't even curse words, she pointed out. My mother began to wring her hands together nervously, avoiding eye contact with her sister. After a little back-and-forth, my mother begged her sister to drop the issue. My aunt pursed her lips and looked sadly over at us girls before eventually taking the CD I had wanted and left the room.

From that point forward, I got sneakier about my reading and music choices. When the *Harry Potter* books started coming out, my grandma sent me the first one and my father made my mother send it back to her. "It's witchcraft, for Christ's sake!" And so of course, it made me want to read the books even more. I concocted an audacious plan with my best friend at school that she would check out the book for me with her library card and I would smuggle the book into my house and read it late at night with a flashlight while everyone was asleep.

My father had begun searching our backpacks when we would get home from school every day. We would come in the front door to the computer desk in the living room, where he was always sitting drinking and playing computer games, and he would go through our backpacks carefully scrutinizing our library book choices, searching for drugs and other satanic and feminist paraphernalia. The day I got the first *Harry Potter* book from my friend, I carefully tucked it into the front of my pants at school and rode the bus home with my big winter jacket on, covering my stomach. I walked in the front door and waited behind my older sister as our father searched her backpack.

When my turn came, I unzipped my bag and stood there cool as a cucumber while my father rifled through its contents, pulling out the two books about Abraham Lincoln I had checked out that day to throw him off my scent. He looked over the books and shoved them back into my bag after a few seconds. "Good. Now go do your fucking homework," he instructed. "Yes, Father," I said, which in recent months had become the mandated response we were required to answer him with or he would hit us because, after all, "Spare the rod, spoil the child," he would say.

I walked slowly to my room, not wanting to seem too eager and raise his suspicion. My entire being tingled with anticipation for what the evening would bring. I hid the book under a pile of junk in my closet and finished my homework and chores. After everyone went to bed that evening, I got out the book and a flashlight I had hidden under my mattress. I pulled my ratty sleeping bag over my head and turned on my flashlight. I read all through the night and entered the wild and wonderful world of *Harry Potter.* I thoroughly believed the book had been written just for me. Harry and I were both born at the end of July, with dark hair and green eyes. We both had scars on our foreheads, and last but certainly not least, both of our families treated us like vermin.

I became so convinced that my letter from Hogwarts was coming, I would volunteer to walk half a mile to our mailboxes daily to check for it. The bad news is, my letter from Hogwarts never came. The good news is, my father fell off the Jesus wagon again. He saw the first *Harry Potter* movie in theaters, and with a flick and a swish we were allowed to start reading the books.

My sweet grandma preordered each book and sent them to me. As each book was released, Harry and I advanced through the same ages and faced a lot of the same problems. While I wasn't the boy who lived, I was facing off with my own personal version of Voldemort at home. And one day, I too would kick his ass.

In the *Harry Potter* books, I found what I believed to be the most epic love story of all time. And no, it wasn't Ron and Hermione, not Harry and Ginny. And although the whispers of allusion to the whirlwind romance between Dumbledore and Grindelwald stirred something deep within me, it was actually Snape's fierce love of Lily that touched my Grinch-sized heart in a profound way. The fact that she seemed to have friend-zoned him to infinity couldn't shake his love for her. She chose someone else, who honestly seemed like kind of a fuck-boy (sorry, not sorry), and yet Snape's love endured. It does seem he respectfully accepted the boundary she set with him. I thought it was so incredibly powerful that despite his love being unreturned, it didn't diminish it. It lasted a lifetime. And it cost him everything.

I have never been so in love with a literary character as I am with Severus Snape. His poetic and mysterious darkness led to a decade-long rollercoaster of wondering whether he was, in fact, a villain in the story. I never cry in movies, or in general, but you bet your ass the waterworks were uncontrollable when he revealed his Patronus in the Deathly Hallows as a doe, the same as Lily's. And even Dumbledore, the man who never missed a thing, was shocked. Snape responded to Dumbledore's questioning if he still loved her, after all that time. And he responded, "Always." From the day I read those words, I have spent my life hoping that one day, someone will love me the way Severus loved Lily. As an adult, I got a tattoo on my ribcage commemorating the effect that one word had on me. It says "Always," the A in the shape of the deathly hallows symbol and the tail of the Y a lightning bolt, to remind myself that if the love isn't Severus Snape level, that shit ain't real. I do believe that those books gave me an endless well of hope that I clung to throughout my childhood, and I will always have a profound gratitude to J. K. Rowling for her otherworldly ability to tell, in my opinion, the greatest story ever told.

My mother went through a blonde phase when I started to get into boy bands. We would always have to tag along with her to the salon. It was usually a different salon every time, as my mother would have to pay with a bad check. While we were at one of her salon appointments, I overheard a woman talking to her stylist about how everyone has three great loves in their lives. No more, no less. I was really excited to meet my mother's next husband. I mean, couldn't really be worse than her current one. I imagined he would be tall, handsome, and rich as hell. And since everyone had three great loves, I would get three husbands too. My first would obviously be Lance Bass. The second would be Bruce Willis because, well, daddy issues. And then I would grow old with Eminem and have two babies and sixteen dogs with him.

In the fourth grade, one of the only things that mattered to me was winning the talent show that year. I had been coordinating a dance routine to "Here We Go" by NSYNC with two of my friends. One day in music class, the teacher was probably feeling particularly hungover, as she told us we could work quietly on our talent show acts. We all split up into our various solo and group acts while our teacher took a nap at her desk. While I was executing a flawless rendition of my knock-off Britney Spears moves, the front office came over the intercom and paged me to the office. The teacher signaled me without even raising her head off the desk. With a snap of her fingers and a flick of the wrist, I knew I was in deep shit.

I figured I was being summoned to the front office for throat-punching Blake Campbell at recess that day. It was going to be super fun explaining that phone call to my drunk father. I was going over my plan to tell my father that it was vigilante justice. I had to do it. Blake had called me a stinky lesbian at recess. I didn't know what that was, but I did know Blake Campbell was a little shit and had it coming. By the time I reached the front office, I had the whole thing worked out in my head. My father said that lesbians go to Hell, so really, I was fighting for Jesus on the playground that day. It was a holy throat punch, kind of like the crusades. I was just about to turn on my deer-in-the-headlights look for Principal Jackson when I was greeted by my mother's best friend Sherry waiting to pick me up at the front office.

She told me my mother had had an accident at the house that day and was in the hospital. Sherry told me my mother would be okay but needed her to pick up us kids from school that day. In the car on the way to Sherry's house, I asked her what had happened to my mom. She told me my mother had been cleaning out a pan of brownies with a knife while we were at school and the knife had slipped and she had accidentally cut both her wrists. I was furious. For one thing, we never got to eat brownies. So what? My mom just made brownies when we were at school and ate them all before we got home? And now I was never going to win the talent show that year because I didn't get to finish practicing my sweet, sweet moves. The truth was, though, that my mother had tried to slit her wrists and had earned herself a 72-hour stay in the friendly local psych ward. I didn't really understand what that meant at the time, but I did know my mother didn't seem quite herself after this. The ensuing downward spiral led to a good amount of confusion, as I was used to my mother being the only consistent star in the macabre circus that was my home life.

After this, my mother spent a few weeks drinking pretty heavily. She started going out to the bars with my father, leaving us at home and stumbling in at all hours of the night. One night in particular, she came home feeling ill and I held her hair back while she vomited in the toilet. I had started gagging too, as I have always had a weak stomach, and she turned around and said, "What's your problem, you little bitch?" I was furious. I had stepped in between her and my father on countless occasions, and taken extra beatings defending her honor. Fucking Judas. In indignation, I dropped her sweat-drenched, bleached-blonde hair out of my hands and said, "You're the bitch, bitch." She started yelling for my father as I scurried out of her bathroom. When I reached the living room, my father asked me what she was going on about. "I don't know, she's not making any sense," I said. "Yeah, your mom can't handle her liquor. Just leave her there." And with that, I was off the hook for calling my mother a bitch. And the cherry on top was that she didn't remember anything the next day.

After briefly trying on alcoholism, my mother stopped drinking and started taking an assortment of anti-psychotic pharmaceuticals. Her lithium-fueled zombie state led to my sister and I having to pick up even more slack around the house. Deb would take baths for hours, refilling the water every couple hours as the water cooled. I would press my ear against the door and listen to her endless sobs. I wanted to fix her so badly. I couldn't understand why she just shut down. Greg was, in my opinion, a shark. Any sign of weakness around him was blood in the water. And he could smell that shit from a mile away. Only then, when you were at your weakest, would he move in for the kill. During my mother's worst bout of depression, Greg threatened to have her "committed." He assured her that she would never see her kids again. Shortly after this, Greg told her that we didn't have the money to keep paying for her medication. Miraculously, Deb drained the bathtub and checked back into life, assuming her old role in our family. And while relieved, I was apprehensive that another brownie incident may be around the corner.

My father was one of seven children. I don't know much about his upbringing, but I can surmise it wasn't ideal. One of his sisters got pregnant when she was twelve, and naturally got married at thirteen. It was a different time, I suppose. My father also had a brother they called Lucky. One night in 1975, my father and his brother were out partying. At the end of the night, my father was driving them home and they got into an accident. Their car rolled seven times and Lucky died from his injuries. I remember thinking it was pretty ironic his name was Lucky, as he didn't seem to be blessed with any. I used to wish that it had been my father who had died in the crash. I would take not being born if it meant my father wasn't living either. I do believe that this accident caused a rift between my father and his siblings, which perhaps motivated his immigration to the States. When I was thirteen, his youngest sister died of a prescription overdose.

We drove up to Canada from Colorado. I had just gotten a CD Walkman for my birthday and the Celine Dion *One Heart* album. When we arrived, I was pleasantly surprised that my father's family seemed pretty awesome. They all had hot tubs and played hockey. Even their missing front teeth seemed oddly endearing. Canada was beautiful. I was under the impression we were traveling to the Arctic, but was relieved that it was late summer there just like back in Colorado. The terrain seemed so much more alive than back home. We drove past picturesque neighborhoods with perfectly manicured lawns and neat rows of divinely green trees. The air was ripe with the scent of freshly cut grass and optimism. That trip was the only time in my childhood I remember my father seeming like an actual human being and not Hitler incarnate. As I shoved ketchup potato chips and Coffee Crisp bars in my face, I listened to my Celine Dion CD on repeat and in that moment, life was pretty good.

The only time I ever saw my father cry was when we were driving away from my aunt's funeral. He was driving the car in silence and started making a choking sound. I thought he was dying too at first, which in my mind would have been ideal. And we were only going like 35 miles per hour, so odds were we would survive the accident that was sure to ensue. However, the sounds morphed into deep guttural sobs and tears suddenly started streaming down his face. "This is all my dad's fucking fault, everything, her overdose, her being a lesbian," he sobbed. And for the first time in my life, I found myself feeling sorry for my captor. I didn't have the heart to ask him if her lesbianism meant she was going to hell. Instead I put my headphones on and listened to Et Je T'aime Encore over and over. It was in that moment that I had an epiphany that has stuck with me to this day. No matter what you are going through in life, there's a Celine Dion song for it.

Chapter 9

This One Time at Band Camp

In the third grade, our music teacher told us that if we wanted to start playing an instrument, we could pick whatever one we wanted and have our parents fill out a form so we could start renting one from a company that would give us the instrument we chose. My sister had already begun playing the flute, and I was supremely jealous of the long silver stick she had been using for the last year to assert her dominance over me. Naturally, I decided I would also play the flute and ultimately defeat her by becoming the best flutist the world had ever known.

Luckily, I caught my father on a good day and he agreed to allow me to pursue my dreams of becoming a flutist. My grandparents agreed to foot the bill, and I signed up for my school's band and joined the ranks of the fourteen other girls who apparently had the same sudden dream as me. I played the flute for six months. During that time, I acquired a taste for the brass section, mostly because of a trumpet player named Marco Brandini. I became convinced that Marco was my soulmate. He had dark brown hair and delicious chocolate-brown eyes that made my soul melt into sweet oblivion every time he looked directly at me. After a while, I decided I had to make a plan to get closer to Marco. Things weren't going well in the flute department anyways. After six months of hard work, I was still only twelfth chair out of fourteen flute players. I decided that I would play the trumpet. I would get to sit next to Marco every day. And obviously we would fall in love and live happily ever after. He was one of only three trumpet players at our school, and I would be the only girl. This was my chance.

I had to first manage to convince my father that I needed to switch to the trumpet. Thus, I began a three-week-long campaign of bringing home library books about Miles Davis and Louis Armstrong, so that when my father conducted my daily backpack search the trumpet seed would already be planted deep in his subconscious. A few weeks into my plan, I asked my father if I could switch from the flute to the trumpet. Conveniently, he had popped a few pain pills before I approached him, which was my favorite of his substance choices, as it always seemed to make him more docile and agreeable. He gave me his permission and my mother called the company I was renting my flute from to let them know I would be switching instruments.

Marco was first trumpet, so I needed to be second trumpet in order to sit next to him. In band, we were tested on our scales every month. We were ranked in our competency based on those tests and given our corresponding chair assignments. First chair was everyone's goal. It was the ultimate achievement. You became the team captain of your section and carried the responsibility of their success in your hands. I personally didn't give two shits about first chair. I needed to be second. I just wanted to sit next to Marco. I was more than happy to have him boss me around.

When I got my new trumpet, I began practicing my scales religiously. I needed to do well on our next test so that I could marry the boy of my dreams. We would start our own little Partridge family, where we would have perfect little babies who would come out of my womb with a trumpet in their hands and their father's magical eyes. My entire life depended on it. When I first joined the ranks of the trumpet section, I was fourth chair and sat next to a boy named Tim who reeked of manure and had a nasty habit of spitting every time he spoke. I didn't care, though. I knew I was on the precipice of all my dreams coming true.

By the time our next scales test came around, I had evolved from practicing intricate scales every night to mastering b-flat versions of all my favorite Disney movie songs in a book of sheet music that my grandmother had sent me. I tested so well that I was awarded the coveted position of first trumpet. I was devastated. And unfortunately, Marco was pissed. Apparently being first chair was very important to him. He never spoke to me again, and told the entire brass and percussion sections that my B.O. smelled like Burger King onion rings.

The funny thing about us Leos is, we don't handle rejection well. Although you would never know, because our prideful, thick exterior makes us seem like nothing phases us. I was beyond devastated that Marco now hated me, but I decided if he was going to hate me I was going to give him a really good fucking reason to. It became my life's mission to become the greatest female trumpet player in the world. I began practicing my trumpet for hours nightly. I beat Marco in every scales test for years.

In middle school, my great-grandmother passed away. I was gutted when my mother told me. The day we got the phone call, I cried in my room for hours, regretting that I hadn't been able to see her for over a year before her passing. There would be no more crochet lessons, no more games of cribbage, no more sun crystal rainbows to put in my pockets. The devastation I felt knowing my favorite woman on the planet existed no more was unparalleled. My father had been drinking that whole day and was elated to hear that one of my mother's relatives had passed. As soon as my mother hung up the phone, he demanded to know what she had left us and how much money we were getting. Turned out we were getting a nominal amount of money and my great-grandmother's Oldsmobile. My father continued to drink throughout the day celebrating the fact that we were getting a new car.

Meanwhile, I sobbed into a pillow on my bedroom floor, mourning the loss of the woman who had taught me so much. At one point, my father came into my room and said we were all going out to dinner, because apparently we could afford it now. I said I didn't feel like going and I asked if I could stay home alone because I was really sad that Grandma died. My father stood over me as I cried quietly on the floor.

"Oh, get the fuck over it, A. J. You weren't even that close to her. If you're not ready to go in ten minutes, I will give you something to fucking cry about." And with that he stormed out of my room. I could hear him continuing to curse me as he walked down the hallway. I pulled myself off the floor and got ready.

We went to the Golden Corral that night. I watched from across the table, disgusted, as my father stuffed his face with prime rib and mashed potatoes, chasing it down with Diet Pepsi he was pouring shooters of Crown into, as the Golden Corral did not serve alcohol at that time. I briefly considered stabbing him in the neck with my steak knife. I looked around the dining room full of senior couples and families with small children. I decided it was against my better judgment to murder my father at the restaurant and there were too many witnesses, so I ate my dinner in silence. I recall wondering if anyone around me could feel the misery radiating off of me. How was it that my suffering was so completely invisible to the world around me?

My father had a great love of all-you-can-eat buffets when I was growing up. Any time we would go to one, all of us children were required to finish at least two full plates so that he got his "money's worth" out of each meal. The night my great-grandmother passed, I was still required to meet the obligatory two-plate minimum. I was so distraught, I had to force each bite down. It didn't even taste like food to me that night, more like vinegar-soaked bites of betrayal toward my grandmother that we were celebrating her death in such an undignified manner.

At one point during the meal, I excused myself to go to the restroom. I had begun to feel ill from the force-feeding I had subjected myself to avoid a beating. I checked to make sure the restroom was empty, which thankfully it was. I made my way to a stall and proceeded to purge my stomach of its contents. As I stuck my finger down my throat, bringing up more and more of the food I had eaten in blasphemy against my great-grandmother, I felt immense relief. When I had nothing left inside me to purge, I leaned my head against the yellowing subway tiles in the stall I was in. The cold tiles soothed my pounding head. I washed my hands and splashed some cold water on my face at the sink. All of a sudden, I was hit by a rush of endorphins that rivaled anything I had ever experienced.

That euphoric rush made a lasting impact on me. From that point forward, I began to force myself to vomit any time I was feeling particularly low. It quickly morphed from a forced activity to a compulsive need to purge anytime my stomach felt full. There was so much in my life that had been outside my control, but my new little habit made me feel as though I exerted a secret power over everything. Bulimia became my imaginary friend that remained on my shoulder throughout the rest of my adolescence, and well into my adult years.

About a week later, we took a road trip to Montana for my great-grandmother's memorial, but mostly to collect my father's prize: the Oldsmobile. She was buried in the same cemetery where my great-uncle was laid to rest after his suicide. At her graveside service, I played "The Old Rugged Cross" on my trumpet, as she was an avid churchgoing woman. She was also a freemason, which I thought was kind of badass. As I finished playing her favorite hymn and made my way back to my seat, I looked over at my great-uncle's headstone. I sat back in my chair that wasn't far from where I had sat with her all those years ago, mourning the loss of her son with her. Was she in a better place now too? Her headstone boasted an epitaph with an excerpt from the John Burroughs poem "Waiting": "Nor time, nor space, nor deep, nor high, can keep my own from me."

I eventually recovered from the sudden loss of my great-grandmother. At a family reunion my mother's family had hosted in honor of her 80th birthday, which was the same day as my eighth birthday, she had bestowed on me a golden locket that had belonged to her mother. After her death, I cut out pictures of her and my great-grandfather and put them in the locket. I wore it on a chain under my shirts every day, convinced that it kept her close to my heart, until my father got his grubby hands on it and pawned it when he needed to support his pain pill addiction. Just in case you were wondering, the Celine Dion song that got me through that mourning period was "Because You Loved Me."

I started my period when I was eleven. It was a most unexpected event, as no one had told me that shit was coming. So naturally, I thought I was dying. I came out of the bathroom and told my sister that I was dying and she informed me that I would not only survive this horrific incident, but that it would happen again every month until I shriveled into an old hag and eventually died. Any remnants of a belief in God I still had fizzled out in that moment. Intelligent design, my ass. If God had intentionally designed women to get the shit end of the stick in every aspect of life, he could go fuck himself for all I cared.

We used pads when we could afford them, but when there were none my sister taught me how to fold toilet paper up in my underwear to get the job done. Tampons were for "whores," according to my father, so we were not permitted to use them.

In the ninth grade, I was accepted into an honor band for the area of the state I was in. It was several hours away from where we lived, so the school paid to put my father and me up in a hotel room for the weekend of the performance. The first night of that weekend, I had gotten my period earlier than I expected and didn't have any pads on hand. Meanwhile, my father had been spending that weekend familiarizing himself with the bars in that area. He left me in the hotel to go out and drink every night until the wee hours of the morning, when he would stumble in and pass out fully clothed in the bed next to mine.

When we checked into our hotel, I realized that our bathroom had come stocked with complimentary tampons. These mysterious instruments of the devil greatly intrigued me. Like, how did you even use them? I needed to know. I spent one of the nights my father was out drinking trying to solve this enduring mystery. I was three tampons in before I finally cracked the Da Vinci Code of menstruation. I was quite proud of myself for teaching myself how to use a tampon. I felt I was finally a real woman. And I realized in that moment that if I could teach myself how to use a tampon, I could teach myself how to do anything.

Chapter 10

Hoop Dreams

I started playing basketball in the first grade. I played on my sister's second-grade team, because they were a player short. Turned out spending my days fighting a grown man and running around a trailer park gave me a competitive edge on the girls who spent their days playing with Barbies and braiding their hair.

It became very obvious that my older sister was more musically inclined than athletic. The kid had the voice of an angel. So she quickly left the basketball court and joined the choir. I, however, remained, much to the delight of Greg.

My father insisted on reminding us daily about how athletic he used to be. He always told us he used to play semi-pro hockey with Wayne Gretzky, which I'm sure was a crock of shit. He quickly became one of those parents who lived vicariously through their children's extracurricular activities. Through elementary and most of middle school, my father volunteered to be our team's coach almost every year.

Despite having *mein fuhrer* as a coach, I did actually really enjoy the game. I was scrappy and fast. And being part of a team got me some new friends, which I was pretty bad at making. I found the better I did on the court, the better things would be at home. Greg had told me that the only way I could go to college was to get a scholarship. And the only way to get a scholarship was to practice every day. I had to be the best, he said. We got a basketball hoop in the backyard, and every day after school and basketball practice I would go to the backyard and practice for a couple hours until the sun went down. I started to channel all my energy into becoming a baller.

My father stopped being my coach after the seventh grade. He got kicked out of a game for cursing out and trying to fight one of the refs after I had fouled out. I'm sure my school had a hand in that, but who knows, maybe he realized it was more socially acceptable to curse at the refs and parents from the other teams more as a spectator than as a coach.

At the end of middle school, Deb got whoopsie pregnant with my youngest brother. My father made me come into the delivery room with them, as he said the experience would be good "birth control" for me. By the time I hit the seventh grade, I was wearing a size D bra, which my father told me made me a target for the boys at my school now. "Guys only want one thing, A. J. Remember that," he would say. Apparently, I was fourteen going on twenty-five. I was not permitted to talk to or even look at boys. So I channeled all my energy into basketball.

I was starting varsity by the ninth grade. During one of my games, I collided with another player who was making her way to the hoop for a layup. Her elbow found its way right into my mouth and shattered one of my front teeth. I asked my father to take me to the dentist the next day. He informed me that if he couldn't afford to go to the dentist, the rest of us didn't stand a chance. It would be two years before I got my tooth fixed. During those two years, I never smiled with my teeth. I ended up getting a part-time job at the daycare my mother worked in a couple days a week and spent six months saving up my paychecks to buy myself a shiny new porcelain veneer. Although a shitty experience, I did learn a level of resourcefulness from that. If I couldn't rely on a man to buy me a new tooth, I could always get a job and buy it for my mother-fucking self.

The girls' basketball team at the public high school I went to didn't really have a history of winning many games, so my father started reaching out to other schools to work on transferring me to one with a more competitive team. And unfortunately, my father was back on the Jesus wagon at this time, so he contacted a private Christian high school about an hour away from the trailer park. They had apparently seen me play and wanted to offer me an "academic scholarship" and my father a job on the maintenance crew, as high schools weren't permitted to scout other players or offer them any compensation to play for their teams. It was a little outrageous I was given such a scholarship, as my performance in the world of academia was mediocre at best. My father also started driving one of the buses for the school, so he would have to go in really early to start his bus route. I, of course, had to tag along. So every weekday morning, we got up at four-thirty and made the hour-long drive to my new school.

Every morning we would arrive, Greg would unlock the gym for me and I was expected to shoot and make at least two hundred shots before school started while he drove his bus route. Most days I would actually shoot, but there were certainly times I ended up taking naps in the women's locker room. I started aggressively weight training with a trainer at the school, running three miles a day and chugging protein shakes like they were the nectar of the gods.

Greg found out that a group of 40+ men met at our school's gym every Sunday morning to play pickup basketball. He told me it was better to train against men, as it would give me an extra leg up on my competition. He asked them if I could join and they said I could try out one Sunday and see if I could keep up with their pace. I guess that tryout went well, as I spent the rest of high school playing every Sunday in what I thought was the geriatric league.

My high school's tuition was very expensive and naturally attracted the wealthiest Christians the city had to offer. I was suddenly thrown into a world of what I thought was insane wealth, while still living in a trailer park. As each student got their driver's license, they would start showing up in new Escalades, lifted Jeeps, and snazzy trucks. I was never allowed to get my license in high school, so I rode with my father every morning in the busted-up maroon Oldsmobile that we had gotten from my great-grandmother when she passed. At that time in my adolescence, I was extremely self-conscious about being poor. I struggled to fit in with the other students, even the ones on my basketball team.

My success on the court seemed to be directly linked to how my father treated me. If I played well, which I usually did, he would be fairly pleasant to me until the next game came around. If I had an off game, or didn't score enough points, I would be in the doghouse for days. I seemed to be stuck between a rock and a hard place when it came to my father and my basketball coach. I would get lectured by my father for not scoring enough and passing too much. And then my coach would lecture me for being a ball hog and encourage me to pass the ball more. It seemed I couldn't win.

One season, my team ended up losing a home game to a school we had won against before. Nothing seemed to land for me that night, and I only scored five points the whole game. After a couple air balls and a dozen missed three-pointers, my coach pulled me out of the game. I think he knew I was fried and needed a break. I could see my father in the stands throwing his hands up when I got pulled from the game. I felt him shooting daggers at me across the court and every time I looked up at him, he made it a point to shake his head at me in disappointment. As the last buzzer sounded, my heart sunk. Losing the game was the easy part. Facing my father's wrath, however, was another story.

Greg and I walked to the car in silence as the last of my teammates trickled out after the game. They invited us to join them for dinner at Chipotle, but my father informed them we couldn't attend due to the long drive home we had to make. Once we got to the car, my father looked over his shoulder to make sure we were alone.

"You will never get a scholarship, A. J. I mean, what the fuck is wrong with you? Five points. Five fucking points! You know what you are, A. J.? An embarrassment. You're an embarrassment to this family. You humiliated me tonight. Hope you're fucking proud of yourself."

Turned out we were not alone. One of the stoner skateboarders from my school had been perched on the steps by the school entrance where we had parked, secretly smoking a cigarette. His name was Devin and like me, he was a fellow outcast at our school. He had long brown hair and wore band tees with ripped jeans, always accompanied by a studded leather jacket. He was on probation and part of his penance was working the concessions at all the varsity basketball games that year, so he had been at all my home games.

After my father was quite finished, Devin popped up from the staircase and walked up to my father and me.

"Hey, A. J.," he said. "Good game tonight. Bummer you guys lost, but hey, can't win 'em all, right?" And with that he proceeded to give me a high-five and then looked coolly over at my father. "Evenin', Mr. Baker." My father said good evening to him through gritted teeth, and we got in the car as I watched him walk away.

"That kid's a fucking psychopath," my father said as we got into the car.

The rest of the drive was silent, and my father sent me to bed without dinner that night for my subpar performance.

I didn't have many friends in high school, and thus the cafeteria every day at lunch was a panic attack. I didn't have a crew to sit with, so most days I ate my lunch in a bathroom stall so no one would see me eating by myself. The day after that game, I was sitting in a stall eating my stale pb & j. I heard someone come into the restroom and occupy the stall beside me. I snuck a peek at the shoes under the stall next to me. They were a very large, battered pair of black Chucks with a "down with the patriarchy" patch hastily sown onto the side nearest me. I'd know those shoes anywhere.

"Devin?" I asked.

"Oh, hey, A. J. What's up?" he answered me.

"What on earth are you doing in the women's restroom?"

"Oh, well, I was supposed to meet one of the cheerleaders in here. She wanted to buy some weed. Although, now that I think about it, I don't think I've seen her all day. She might be sick. Was Heather in your English class today?"

I was slightly horrified, but mostly intrigued. I was always told that marijuana was the devil's lettuce. My father had told us it was a gateway drug. Apparently you'd smoke it one time, and next thing you know you're a crack whore with six baby daddies. I also couldn't believe that my school's perfect head cheerleader was in the habit of buying drugs in the bathroom.

"Well, shit, man," he laughed. "Guess I should head out. Here, take this. On the house, babe."

I saw his hand slip under my stall with a little plastic baggy containing a bundle of what appeared to be some kind of sticky oregano.

"Devin, I don't know. I'm not even sure what to do with that."

"Oh, shit. Okay, here." He pulled his hand back and I heard him rifling through his pockets. When his hand reemerged, he was holding what appeared to be a hand-rolled cigarette. "This one's easier for beginners."

"Right. Thanks," I said, and took the joint from him.

"Best to pair it with some gum and eyedrops if you are trying to be stealthy. Might want to change your clothes after you smoke too."

"Right, okay. Thanks." I looked down at the joint and contemplated whether all those years of D.A.R.E. and "Just Say No" were all for naught. Would Heather and I become crack whores together? I was debating just giving it back to him when I heard him exit his stall. He knocked on mine.

I stood up and opened it. He looked down at the half-eaten sandwich in my hand.

"Hey, um, A. J? Why don't you sit with us at lunch tomorrow? Also, I, uh, heard everything your dad said to you last night. He seems like a real prick. I'm sorry. My dad's a prick too. Keep your head up, though, we don't have to deal with this shit for much longer, you know?"

"Oh. Yeah. Well, thanks," I said, blushing.

He reached out and tucked a piece of my hair behind my ear. My heart almost leapt out of my chest. And with that, he turned around and exited the women's restroom.

That night, after my father had passed out drunk and everyone went to bed, I climbed out my bedroom window onto the roof of the trailer. I had pilfered a lighter out of a kitchen drawer earlier that day. I lit up the joint and started smoking it as I looked up at the stars. How was it the world was so big and yet mine seemed so small? I thought about what Devin had said, about how we didn't have to put up with our fathers for too much longer. I would soon be an adult. It was the first time I saw a light at the end of the tunnel. In a few short years, I could escape out from under my father's iron fist. One day, I would be free. After I smoked about half the joint, I left it on the roof under a rock in a plastic bag. I did my best to climb silently back into my room and lay in my bed staring at the ceiling.

Once the effects set in, I was initially overwhelmed by a wave of paranoia. I was convinced I was going to get found out and my father would finally murder me for becoming a drug addict. As I waited with baited breath for my father to come storming into my room and bludgeon me to death, I realized I didn't really care. He could kill me if he wanted. I'd probably be better off. Thankfully, the paranoia wore off, and a feeling of euphoria set in. I had never felt anything like this before. It was glorious. My entire being felt like a sweet, creamy, weightless jelly, and in that moment I had not a care in the world. I wasn't used to life feeling good, but whatever Devin had given me had accomplished the impossible. Maybe I could make it through the next couple years after all.

I started sitting with Devin and his friends almost every day at lunch from that point forward and Devin would give me more weed from time to time. I tried to pay him, but he would never accept my money. We made out in the bathroom at school a few times, but ultimately decided we made better friends than lovers. We remained close friends until after I graduated high school, after which he became addicted to harder drugs and faster women, and we eventually lost touch.

Our basketball team managed to win two district championships during my time there. My father would drive my team's bus to each game. I often felt there was no corner of the world safe from my father's grasp. I would sit all the way in the back of the bus and read my *Harry Potter* books to avoid having to converse with him. When we won the district championship my junior year, the parents and fans flooded the court and cheered as all the players cut down a piece of the net. My father cut in front of two of my teammates to cut down a piece as well. He informed bystanders that he was the bus driver, and thus no one would have won the game if he hadn't driven us there safely. I remember wanting to crawl out of my skin, I was so embarrassed. After districts, we went to state every year but would ultimately lose during the first round of the tournament, until my senior year, when we would lose in the second.

That year, my father hit me for the last time. It was during the fall. I had gotten in an argument with my mother and sister on a drive home from the grocery store and ultimately cussed the both of them out. When we arrived home, I stormed down the hallway to my bedroom and plopped myself on my bed. I could hear my mother's raised voice as she told my father what I had said to them. Moments later, I heard my father's thundering steps as he made his way down the hall. He came in holding one of my youngest brother's toy golf clubs.

"Get up," he instructed.

"No," I said.

He whipped the golf club in his hand up behind his head and starting beating me with it. "You don't get to tell me no, you little bitch!"

I jumped out of my bed and ripped the golf club out of his hand. He responded by punching me in the side of the face. I saw red. I made a quick judgment call that after my years of intensive training, I was now strong enough to smoke this mother-fucker. That day, I chose violence. I wound up, and punched my father back twice in the face. Left hook. Right hook. His eyes widened and he stumbled backwards into the doorway of my bedroom, where the hole from the Barney incident still gaped, and for the first time in my life I saw fear in his eyes. He took another swing at me. I dodged the blow and instinctively dished out another left hook that cracked his nose as it connected with his face. That one sent him to the floor.

Something within me snapped that day. Today, it still scares me how much rage I unleashed on that man. I stood over my father and kicked him in the stomach repeatedly until he was gasping for air and he tried yelling out for my mother. I threw in three more solid kicks in rapid succession for good measure. I leaned over him with the devil in my eyes and said, "If you ever touch me again, I will fucking kill you, you hear me, you fat fuck? I'll fucking kill you!" He coughed, holding his nose that was now gushing blood on my bedroom floor.

I ran to the front of the trailer and found my mother crouched on the kitchen floor shaking like an abused rescue dog in a shelter. I told her to pack up her things and get my siblings to do the same. I informed her we were leaving and we were going to drive to my grandparents' house. She just kept shaking and shook her head no. I looked down at her and said, "If you don't leave with me right now, the second I turn eighteen I will leave this house, and you will never see me again."

"I can't leave, A. J.," she said, breathless on the floor.

I walked out the front door and ran down the dirt road all the way to the highway. After a while, I reached a little house that was situated right off the road. I knocked on the door and asked the woman who lived there if I could use her phone to call the police. She guided me inside to the phone. I called 911 and told them that we were being abused and someone needed to help us get out of that house. The woman let me wait there until the police arrived. Unfortunately, I had given the police my home address and so they had gone straight to the trailer instead of the house I had called from. Rookie mistake.

An officer came to collect me from the woman's home and drove me back down the dirt road to the trailer. The officer asked me what happened and I told him everything that had happened that afternoon. I added the abuse had been going on for years and my mother was too scared to leave. One of my biggest regrets is not telling him about the sexual abuse, which I still didn't fully understand at the time. The officer then informed me that they had gotten a much different story from my parents. He added that my father was beat up pretty bad. The officer said the good news was my father didn't want to press charges against me.

When we arrived back at the trailer, my mother and father were sitting on the couch side by side, suddenly dressed like they were headed to church. My father did have a bruised face and was holding toilet paper on his bloody, broken nose. The officer who had driven me back to our house proceeded to give me a lecture about where troubled teens end up and he said I was extremely lucky that my parents weren't pressing charges against me for assaulting my father. I told them that it was fucked up they didn't even look at my body for bruises and showed them the fresh ones I had gotten in the golf club beating. I argued it was self-defense. My father interjected, "Those are old. They are from a basketball tournament. A. J. is a pathological liar." My mother sat next to him the entire time, nodding her head in agreement to everything he said. I glared at my mother from across the room. She wouldn't even look at me. I plopped down on a chair and folded my arms. By this point in my life, I knew a lost cause when I saw one. The officer offered my parents some advice on how to handle their "troubled daughter," and after a few minutes he walked out the door. That day, my mother became public enemy number two to me. Any pity I had for her over the years went out the door forever, just like the policeman. She had chosen this misery for us, and I had offered her a ticket to freedom with my newfound strength and all she did was spit it back in my face.

I got up and went to my room. I listened to my parents discuss my fate for a while. They debated sending me to live with my grandparents, putting me in counseling, or sending me to Canada to live with an aunt. That night, I climbed out my window and slept in a sleeping bag on the roof of the trailer, just in case my father was feeling homicidal after getting his ass kicked.

They did send me to Christian counseling for a while. Greg quickly realized that was a mistake, as my counselor immediately started recommending family sessions, which my father had no interest in attending and insisted that I was the only problem in our household. My last session with the counselor, she said she was concerned about signs of abuse she was recognizing and said she would be reporting it, as she was a mandated reporter, whatever the fuck that meant.

One afternoon about a month later, I had worked a shift at the daycare. I had gotten paid that day and had gone to the bank across the street to cash my check before my father picked me up. I had gotten in the habit of keeping all my earnings in cash on me at all times, as my father had emptied my piggy bank multiple times to fund his drinking and pill habit. Things had been quite tense in our house since I Mike Tyson-ed my father, and I was not looking forward to the drive home. He pulled into the parking lot and I got in the front passenger side. Greg looked straight ahead and said, "Give me your check. You are going to start paying rent to live under my roof."

"Yeah, I'm good on that, thanks," I responded.

He looked over at me and sneered. "You have nowhere to go, and guess what, no one believes you anymore. You can call the police as much as you want, but I promise you, they will take my side. Now you're just a bad kid on paper. Give me the fucking check, A. J. Don't make this any harder than it needs to be. You will lose basketball forever, you little shit."

"Go fuck yourself, Greg." And with that, I jumped out of the car and sprinted through alleys and backroads, sure my father would be ripping after me to hit me with the car, and somehow the police would think that was my fault too. I ran until I couldn't breathe anymore, and looked around. I was not being followed. I powered off the magenta Razor I had purchased a few months earlier and I started walking to the mall I knew was just a couple miles away. As I walked, I contemplated what my life on the lam was going to look like. Basketball was over, and now I was homeless. I would have to get a new job where my father couldn't find me.

I had just secretly watched my parents' pirated VHS copy of *Striptease* with Demi Moore the previous week while home sick from school, and it really got the wheels turning for me. I decided I was hot enough to be a stripper, and that was the best way to stack cash until I could get on my feet. I would lie about my age. And strippers used fake names anyways, so no one would find me. I decided I needed to be blonde to complete this mission.

I went into a salon in the mall and they just so happened to take walk-ins. Four hours later, I left the salon looking like stripper material. I decided I would need new clothes too. I popped into Hollister and chose an ensemble I was sure made me look more grown up. After my transformation was complete, I headed to Barnes and Noble to kill some time and plot my next move. I bought a coffee and a romance novel and sat at one of the tables to read.

I pulled my cell phone out of my pocket and powered it on. I was sure by this time someone would have heard I ran away and would have reached out. I turned my phone back on and waited to see if I had any messages. Greg had texted me that I had been reported as a runaway, the police were looking for me, and that I was in deep shit. I was about to embrace another opportunity to tell him to get fucked, but as I was typing my response out I got a phone call from my assistant basketball coach. I sent it to voicemail and put my phone down. She called three more times and then texted me asking where I was and if I was okay. I was interrupted from watching my phone get blown up on the table by a man asking if he could sit at my table. I nodded.

"My name is Paul. What's yours?" he asked, as he sat down across from me.

"Brooke," I said, convinced this was my opportunity to create my new identity.

"That's a pretty name. I couldn't help noticing you sitting over here by yourself. You're gorgeous. Sorry, I hope I'm not being too forward. Do you have a boyfriend?"

I studied the stranger in front of me. He looked like he was old enough to be my dad. He was tall, handsome, and had brown hair and blue eyes. Wrinkles had just started to set in on his forehead.

"No, I don't," I told him. I'd never had a boyfriend.

He started talking to me again, but I was distracted by the buzzing of my phone with another text from my coach: "Please just let me know you're okay." I responded that I was okay and she immediately asked where I was. I set the phone down again, feeling like an idiot for blowing my cover a few short hours into my escape.

"Well, perfect," he said. "Would you like to grab dinner with me sometime?"

"Sure." I picked my phone back up and responded to my coach's text, saying I didn't want to tell her where I was because I didn't want my father to know.

The man and I talked for a while and when I had finished my coffee, he went up and ordered me another one. He proceeded to sit with me for the next hour, asking me about myself. I was sure that if he found out I was only sixteen, he would jump up from the table like he had just sat on napalm. When he finally did ask me how old I was, I told him I was eighteen. He told me he was forty-four and asked me if that was weird. I said no. Over the course of the conversation, my coach kept texting me begging for a response. She told me she could come get me, wherever I was, and she wouldn't tell my father where I was. She offered to let me crash at her house for the night, and promised me we could just worry about everything in the morning. I eventually told her where I was and she responded she was on her way.

At one point the man asked me if I was in any trouble. He noticed I seemed upset and kept nervously checking my phone. I said I was fine and was just waiting on a friend to pick me up. He offered to give me a ride somewhere but I declined. He asked me for my phone number before my "friend" arrived. We continued to talk and our conversation evolved into deeper topics. When he asked me about my family, I told him about my father being a monster and he genuinely looked sad to hear it. He reached under the table and put his hand on my thigh. I started to regret revealing my location to my coach. Maybe this guy wasn't so bad. He seemed to really care that I was going through some shit and he was pretty fucking hot.

Right as I was contemplating leaving the bookstore with the man before my coach arrived and riding off into the sunset with my new daddy/boyfriend, my coach walked in the front door. The relief on her face upon seeing me at the table instantly turned into reprehension as she saw the older man sitting with me. Realizing this was the friend I had been waiting for, he stood from the table and reached out to shake her hand.

"Hi, I'm Paul," he said.

She looked down at his hand like it was covered in dog excrement and responded without shaking his hand, "She's sixteen. Get your things, A. J. Let's go, girlfriend."

My face flushed as I was outed to my new love for lying about both my name and my age.

"Sorry, I have to go," I said to him.

I grabbed my bag and my new book and left with my coach. She took me to her house, where she ordered us pizza and we watched *10 Things I Hate About You.* She set me up in her guest room and I turned in for the night. I wasn't able to sleep, as I was nervous about what the next day had in store for me. My small taste of freedom would soon be over, and I would have to face the wrath of my father yet again.

Around one in the morning, Paul texted me and asked if I was okay. I said yes. He then told me it didn't bother him that I was only sixteen and that I seemed very mature for my age. We texted all night.

The next morning, my coach drove me to school, where I was called into the office during first period. I was directed back to the athletic director's office. He was also the head coach of my basketball team. My father was also sitting in the office. He didn't look at me when I walked in. I sat down and braced myself for what I was sure would be my immediate expulsion for running away.

My coach looked me up and down and said, "Nice hair. Your father and I are really worried about you. Running away like that could have ended so much worse. I mean, what's going on with you, A. J.? What were you thinking?"

I looked over at my father, who still wasn't making eye contact with me. "I don't know. I just needed to get away, Coach. My father tried to take my paycheck and make me pay rent to live at home. I'm just done with this. I can't live like this anymore. He's horrible to us and no one will do anything to stop him."

My father then interjected. "That's enough of that. Your coach is already aware of your behavior issues and no one is buying this little act of yours. Things are going to change from here on out. I've written up a behavioral contract and if you want to continue playing basketball and going to school here, you're going to sign it. And if you step out of line again, the consequences will be severe. You've also been reported to the police as a runaway, so after this, we will be going to the police station to let them know you're no longer missing."

I looked at my father in disbelief. "Are you fucking serious right now? I'm not signing anything. This is so fucked up."

"Language, A. J.," my coach said calmly. "Look, kid, you don't have to sign anything right now, okay? Let's just get you over to the guidance counselor's office. You can talk to her a bit, and then she can drive you over to the police station to get all that squared away."

I think he was as surprised as I was when my father whipped out the contract he had typed up. My father interjected that I didn't need to go to the counselor's office and that he would be taking me to the police himself.

"A. J., can you give us the room for a minute, kiddo?" my coach said.

I stepped out and made my way to the guidance counselor's office.

I spent the next hour in the counselor's office begging her to help me. She was a beautiful, tall blonde woman who radiated confidence. She was everyone's favorite staff member, as she had a habit of letting any student who was going through some shit hang out in her office during class and eat out of the giant jar of candy she always kept fully stocked on her desk. I told her about why I had run away and about what a violent drunk my father had always been. She took some notes and finally packed up her things and told me she'd drive me to the police station. Before we left, she gave me the entire jar of candy that she kept on her desk for the drive.

When we arrived at the front desk of the police station, we were greeted by a large female officer who reminded me of a pale middle-aged version of Violet Beauregarde after she blew up like a giant berry in the *Charlie and the Chocolate Factory* novel. Her shirt buttons were bursting at the seams in a way that made it seem like they'd rather kamikaze pop into oblivion than remain on her bulbous frame for another second. I could certainly relate to the buttons.

As we walked in, the woman stood up from her seat at the front desk. I was shocked at how tall the woman was. She placed both her arms on her hips and looked down at me in disdain. "You must be A. J. Your father has told me all about you. You need to realize something, honey. You have good, hardworking parents who are doing the best they can for you. And just because you don't get your way all the time doesn't mean you can just run off every time you feel like it. And it just so happens—"

My counselor cut her off, her gorgeous blonde hair moving in unison with her head as it jetted from side to side. "Well, that is certainly a lot to assume before you've even talked to this young woman, Officer. Just out of curiosity, would you offer her the same advice if you knew she was being abused? Which, I guess, as a legally mandated reporter, I am obliged to report that I have sufficient cause to believe, and I need to report that to you or perhaps someone less biased and more qualified who is available for me to speak with."

The giant police officer's jaw dropped, and she let out a sound that imitated what I imagined a goose would make in its final moments as it was guillotined for a Christmas feast. The two woman glared at each other, and just as I thought the larger woman would swallow my poor counselor whole, two male police officers walked around the corner followed closely by my father. I was subsequently fingerprinted and photographed "just in case" I pulled a stunt like that again. After I had been thoroughly humiliated, one of the male police officers asked to speak with me privately in an interrogation room. My father tried to say that wouldn't be necessary and I would just waste their time with more of my lies. The female officer once again interjected that she saw this type of thing all the time and didn't appreciate my counselor's attitude and disrespect for the badge. I told them I would like to speak with an officer and pulled out a business card for the other counselor my parents had sent me to after I beat the daylights out of my father. "Please call my therapist," I said. "Even she said she recognized patterns of abuse."

"She's not her counselor anymore," my father quickly stated.

"Okay, honey, well, when was the last time you visited this therapist?" one of the male officers asked me.

"Two days ago," I said.

The male officer, who was a balding older man with a salt-and-pepper mustache and gentle brown eyes, gave my father a look that gave me hope someone might actually believe me for once. He then guided me to a room down the hall from the front desk. Once inside, he asked me if I wanted anything to drink. I said no thank you. He informed me that my counselor was putting up a good fight for me.

"Here's the deal, though, sweetheart. I believe you that your father is unkind and probably is doing things that aren't okay to y'all. I've only spent twenty minutes with him and I'm not too fond of him myself. But your mother has backed him on everything he's said. My hands are pretty tied. We work within the confines of the law, and because of that, unless you had walked in here all bruised to hell and your father had beaten you to within an inch of your life, there's not much we can do. If he does hit you and you get bruises, though, please call me. I would love to help you, darling, but I have to follow the laws, and as of right now the law gives parents a lot of freedom to discipline their children as they see fit. If he tells you to use your toothbrush to scrub out the toilet and then makes you brush your teeth, you still have to do it. We really only take people's children away when their lives are actually in danger."

Tears started spilling down onto my cheeks as I listened to the officer who, only moments before, I believed would be my ticket to freedom. He put his hand on my shoulder.

"Here's the silver lining, though, kiddo. You're sixteen. You only have a couple more years left and then boom, you're free. And you know what, once you turn seventeen, you could even legally emancipate yourself. You just have to prove you're of sound mind and can support yourself. And that's, what, only six months away. Stop running away, though; it doesn't look good on your record if you are going to pursue emancipation. Hang in there, kiddo. This is only temporary."

He walked across the room and got me a box of tissues. He waited for me to stop crying, and then I followed him out of the room and back out to the front entrance. My counselor said she'd see me at school the next day and then gave my father a dirty look as I walked behind him to the car. The good news is he spent the next month pretending I didn't exist, I never signed his "contract," and I was still permitted to play basketball.

I spent the next few months texting back and forth with the older man from the coffee shop. We would exchange nudes from time to time, but I eventually lost interest. I think I really just got sick of looking at pictures of his erect penis next to soda cans for scale. I knew we'd never be able to have an actual relationship because I was still in my domestic prison for a couple more years. I stopped responding to his messages until he finally gave up.

The next year was mostly uneventful. My father spent most nights in the bars or passed out on pain pills, and I avoided him at all costs. I played basketball and kept my head down, counting down the days until freedom.

Toward the end of my senior basketball season, I was approached by two scouts for small colleges, both in Nebraska. I was offered partial scholarships to both schools. I was also offered a scholarship to play in the concert band at a small college in Indiana. My father informed me that I was going to be accepting the scholarship from the school in Nebraska that was closest to Colorado. I told him that I would not be accepting any scholarships and was done playing basketball. I decided I was going to be spending my college years experiencing everything I had been robbed of enjoying in my adolescence. After I told him that, he clenched his jaw and his face began to turn a deep shade of purple as he raised his arm like he was going to hit me. I squared up. I was very serious about my threat to kill my father if he ever laid hands on me again. I smiled at him.

"So today's the day you meet your maker, huh, mother-fucker? I have nothing left to lose. Take a swing," I said to him as I raised my fists.

He chewed on my words for a moment as his lower jar continued to shake, the fat on his jowls shuddering like a soft child who had just been exorcised of a demon. He lowered his hand.

"You know what? You're not even worth my time, you little bitch. What a fucking waste of space you are. Enjoy life as a crack whore. One day you'll look back on this moment and realize it was the biggest mistake of your fucking life." He walked away.

I flipped him off behind his back and laughed to myself. It was in that moment that I realized his power over me was dwindling and his days of tyranny were numbered.

The scouts continued to come to my games until my final game at state my senior year.

After that last game, I didn't exist to my father anymore. He ignored me whenever I spoke to him, so I finally stopped speaking to him altogether. My mother would relay any messages from him regarding pickup and drop-off times for school. For the first time in my life, the dark oppressive cloud hanging over me that was my father was starting to blow away. I found a glimmer of hope for my life beyond the confines of my father's grip and began testing the limits of my newfound freedom.

Chapter 11

Smoke 'Em if You Got 'Em

Once my basketball days were over and I realized my father knew I was serious about my threat to kill him, I stopped listening to anything he told me
to do. He could no longer hold taking basketball away from me over my
head. However, with my newfound free time and lack of friends, I found
myself in a deep bout of depression I wasn't prepared for. Basketball had
been the entire purpose of my life for so long that in its absence I felt like I
was worthless.

My senior year, we had moved from the trailer park into the city, where
my high school was. We rented a house from one of my mother's coworkers at
the daycare. It seemed like a mansion to me at the time but it was, in fact, just
an average suburban home. Complete with a finished basement, sunken living
room, and a large upstairs, I was relieved to finally escape trailer park life.

My sister had just gotten a sizable vocal scholarship at a college four
hours away and I was now the oldest child at home. I went through a two-
week period where I couldn't get out of bed. My father would pound on my
locked bedroom door in the morning, summoning me to get in the car for
school. I would sometimes say I was sick or usually just ignore him.

"What, so now we're a high school fucking dropout? Enjoy working
at McDonald's," he would say before eventually giving up and leaving
without me.

"At least I'd have a real job, fuck-face," I'd say just quiet enough so he
couldn't hear me.

After everyone left, I would go down to the basement, where my sister's
old bedroom was, and lay on her floor for hours. During that time, I started
to envy the dead baby from the trailer park years before. Perhaps the best
life for people like the baby and me was no life at all. He got off easy. Suffocating on a blanket seemed like a cakewalk compared to the seventeen years
of torture I'd endured. I'd spend hours brainstorming the best way to off
myself but couldn't seem to put any plans into motion. After a while, I would

pull myself off the floor and walk a mile to the nearest Starbucks for a black coffee. One day I went in to get my coffee, and the guy who was working behind the counter looked oddly familiar. Turned out he had graduated from my high school a few years before me.

"Shouldn't you be in school, A. J.?" he asked me.

"Oh. Yeah, um, I'm kind of on vacation, I guess," I said as he handed me the coffee he wouldn't let me pay for.

"Nice," he said, smiling at me, his mystical blue eyes glaring deep into my soul.

I came in every day for a week while he was working, and he eventually asked me for my phone number. We started texting all the time, and he helped me bounce back from the depression that was plaguing me. He started picking me up after school most days, and we would drive around listening to Coldplay and talking about life. He was attending a local community college and constantly bitched about his parents and his feelings.

After a couple finger-banging trysts, and perfecting my blow job technique, I grew weary of his constant outpouring of emotions. Since basketball had ended, my favorite form of cardio had become running from my feelings and I didn't really want to deal with anyone else's. I think he also didn't enjoy dating someone who was dead inside. So we eventually broke things off and I went back on spending my days on my sister's bedroom floor.

Ultimately, my absences led to academic issues. Faced with the threat of not graduating, I returned to school. One day while sitting with Devin and his friends at lunch, another girl joined our table. Her name was Britney and she was the first-chair flute in our band. I was first trumpet out of twenty-two so I had been around her regularly, especially in our monthly band meetings, where all the first chairs would gather with our conductor and complain about the cretins we had below us who weren't carrying their weight in our sections as we prepared for nationals. We hadn't really spoken much, though, as I assumed her love of Abercrombie and perfect orthodontics lumped her in with all the other preppy rich fucks from my school who lacked the substance I so desperately craved.

She had started dating one of the emo kids who sat at our rejects table, so I assumed I would just have to get used to her. The guys were deep in debate about their various World of Warcraft opinions while Britney and

I started to look around in boredom. We started talking, and turned out Britney was pretty fucking cool. Her father was a chiropractor, and her parents held her to a preppy pretty princess standard she didn't care to meet anymore. I guess she had a different kind of daddy issues, as she found herself falling for a guy who was the exact opposite of what her parents envisioned for her.

She started inviting me over to her house for sleepovers on the weekends. I was never allowed to have sleepovers or go to other people's houses up until this point, and the concept fascinated me. I had stopped asking for permission to do things anymore and started informing my mother of my weekly plans so she could relay them to my degenerate father, who had seemed to lose the will to fight me since I had broken his nose and ribs. It was an opportunity to escape my home for a short while and I seized it.

We would spend a lot of weekends at the mall with her daddy's credit card and then in her bedroom giggling as we debated who our hottest teachers were. She was sweet on our new history teacher. He was still in his early twenties and while I agreed that his display of swordsmanship he used one day to explain the whole Istanbul and Constantinople situation was pretty hot, I was more attracted to our Bible teacher in his fifties with a receding hairline and delicious dark chocolate-brown eyes that reminded me of the mochas my barista ex-boyfriend preferred to drink. He was softspoken and compassionate. And there was something about his dad bod that really got me. I also got really hot and bothered over the idea of corrupting such a holy man.

Britney tried to hide her horror as I revealed my faculty crush to her. Being a good friend, she laughed it off and said, "Well, at least we'll never fight over a guy."

The woman we rented our new house from lived right around the corner from us with her adult son. They were odd birds. They were both quite short with even shorter arms that didn't seem to be proportional to their bodies. Whenever my mom's coworker/landlord would come to the front door to ask why they hadn't paid the rent, my father would mock them after they left, shortening his arms and waving them around dramatically as he listed all the reasons why they were bad landlords and they were lucky that we paid them at all.

One day my mother instructed me to run what I'm sure was a bad check over to their house. I knocked on their front door and the woman's son answered. He invited me inside the house and proceeded to tell me that his mother wasn't home. In his slow, stuttered speech, he asked me if I wanted a beer.

"Fuck it. Sure," I said.

He brought me a Bud Light and cracked one open for himself. "I want to show you something," he said.

I chugged my very first beer down, noting that it tasted like carbonated piss. I followed the man into his mother's basement, wondering if he was planning on murdering me. All my years of watching *Forensic Files* had taught me I was probably walking into a trap. I wasn't too intimidated, though. I was still bench-pressing 120 at the time and he was about half the weight of my father. The man seemed much too docile to put up a good fight against the seventeen years of pent-up rage I had swirling around inside of me.

When we got to the bottom of the stairs, I was amazed to see that the entire basement was occupied by a giant Lego spaceship.

"Holy shit, man! Did you build this?" I asked him.

"Yep," he said, beaming, as he held his hands on his hips, looking like Buzz Lightyear about to blast off into infinity.

It was big enough to be an actual spaceship. I was amazed. Once every couple weeks, I started coming over to their house and drinking beers with him for hours while he worked on his spaceship. I'm pretty sure his mother never evicted us for our months of unpaid rent because I started having Lego playdates with her forty-two-year-old son. We didn't tell her about the beer, though. Besides Devin and Britney, he was one of my best friends in high school.

The week after my high school graduation, my aunts planned a family reunion in Durango. They had booked cabins for everyone and had a plan for everyone to pay a chunk of the costs. My father hated my aunts and decided a great way to avoid paying for the cabins was to camp at a nearby campground and pitch a tent in defiance of their carefully curated reunion plans.

On the drive up, my father informed us children that we would all be camping with him and were not to stay in the cabins. I rolled my eyes. I was thirty days away from turning eighteen and had already been making an exit strategy. I had been squirreling away cash from my job at the daycare and various babysitting gigs. I was planning on getting a car, my driver's license, and moving out the second I turned eighteen.

When we got to Durango, we set up the campsite and headed over to the cabins to see my mother's family. We exchanged hugs and pleasantries upon arrival. I always got a kick out of watching my father have to hug my aunts. The loathing was seeping out from underneath all their forced smiles. One of my aunts moved in to hug him so aggressively, I thought she was going to strangle him. I waited, hoping she would, imagining myself stepping in to help her finish the job. Instead, she reached out one arm and awkwardly pulled him in for a firm side hug.

She was made aware of our accommodations at the campground. She looked over at my father and pursed her lips.

"Well, the kids are welcome to stay here. That was the plan all along, as I'm sure you remember, Greg. What do you think, kids? You wanna sleep here with us?" she said, smiling over at me.

"Absolutely!" I said, running to the back of the car to grab my duffel bag.

No one else from my family accepted the invitation. I looked over at Father, clenching his teeth. I knew he wouldn't say shit to me in front of my mother's family, and he knew what fate awaited him if he laid another finger on me, so I was off the hook.

That night, two of my cousins invited me on a late-night walk with them. We walked down the side of the road, looking up at the stars. They pulled out a joint and started to smoke it. As they offered it to me, I declined. I didn't give a fuck what my father thought anymore, but I didn't want my aunts to find out and think I was a degenerate. My cousin shrugged as he turned Eazy-E on a small battery-operated boombox he had brought along. He looked over at me.

"You're too wound up, A. J. You gotta chill, you know, man? Smoke 'em if you got 'em, that's my motto," he said as he took a long drag off of the joint.

I envied his carefree spirit. I wanted to tell them how lucky they were to have my aunt as a mother, where the only consequences for getting caught smoking a joint would have been a stern lecture, unlike myself, where before I had taken an aggressive power stance, I was at risk of being murdered by my guardian.

The week I turned eighteen, I did, in fact, execute my plan of getting a car and my license. I had enrolled to go to college in the town we lived in. I had been filling out paperwork for student loans on the downstairs computer one evening. I must have left it up on the computer when I went to bed, as my father saw it and started making a plan of his own.

I came downstairs the next morning ready to go buy my books for my upcoming semester when I was greeted by my father at the kitchen table drinking a glass of whiskey.

"We need to talk," he said.

"Um, okay, but it needs to be quick. I have plans this morning," I answered.

He frowned. "I saw what you were doing on the computer last night. You are going to put me on that new bank account of yours so I can monitor your spending," he said.

I had seen him ruin my sister's credit by taking out a cable account in her name after she turned eighteen because they wouldn't let him have an account, as he had a "history" with them.

I laughed at him. "Yeah, no. I will not be doing that. Thanks, though," I said.

He slammed the glass of whiskey on the table, spilling some on the past-due notices piling up on the table underneath his glass.

"Then get your shit and get the fuck out of my house!" he screamed at me.

I flipped him a double bird and said, "Gladly." I had also seen him pull this shit on my sister before. Where my sister was always the peacekeeper and caved, giving into his wishes, I had fought him every chance I had for eighteen long years, and I certainly wasn't done fighting now. I wasn't scared of living in my car. Better homeless than stuck in that hellhole in my mind. I called his bluff, not giving a single fuck what the consequences might be.

He got up from the table and grabbed his car keys. He left in silence and headed for the bar.

While he was at the bar that day, I proceeded to pack all my belongings into my car. As I left the house with the last load, I looked around the living room. All the echoes of years of screams and broken glass felt suffocating. I shuddered and walked out the front door. After I packed the last load, I got into the driver's seat. I took a deep breath. Tears welled up in my eyes as I put the car into first gear. I had no idea where I was going or what the fuck I was doing, but I knew I was finally free. I pulled my favorite CD out and started playing "That's The Way It Is" by Celine Dion. And with that, I drove off into the sunset and never looked back.

Chapter 12

Silver Linings

While growing up in the Church, I often heard people say that God will never give you more than you can handle. I always thought that was a crock of shit, but now I think it's just a nice thing people say to help you feel strong enough to make it through whatever it is you're going through. I walked away from the Church when I was nineteen and never looked back. I realized that I do, in fact, like Jesus and all he stood for; it's just his fan club that gets in the way. I do believe there is something bigger at work, but I don't think it's a one-size-fits-all situation.

For a long time, I never spoke about my trauma and sexual abuse. I was embarrassed about where I came from. I felt like it made me dirty. I didn't think men would want to be with me if they knew I had been damaged in that way by my father, like I was used goods. I didn't want the world to see my ugly scars, so I hid them as best I could. It took me until I was almost thirty to realize that was bullshit. It is not our past that defines us. It shapes us, for sure, but it doesn't hold our worth. I spent a long time being a victim of circumstance, and it wasn't until I realized we all hold the pen to our own stories that I came into my power as a strong, independent woman.

I've heard it said that your trauma is not your fault, but the healing is your responsibility. I wish I could tell you that the second I turned eighteen I won the lottery and rode off into the sunset with Eminem, but it was a long, hard road processing through my trauma and taking it out on the world around me for a good while. My Band-Aids became bulimia, drugs, alcohol, and sitting on a pile of dicks. I did, however, slowly start to seek a better way. Through years of specialized therapy, a dark sense of humor, and micro-dosing psilocybin, I have learned to manage my PTSD and laundry list of issues caused by my childhood.

I cut off all ties with my nuclear family after 2008 and didn't start talking to them again until the death of my father in June of 2019. He died of kidney disease-related heart failure. At the end of his rope, and staring his mortality in the face, he made a suicide pact with my mother so they could be "together forever." Thankfully, my mother never carried out her end of the deal. She understandably has a good amount of trauma and mental illness from her long, hard life. I have finally found it in myself to forgive her for her role in this story. She was, after all, just a baby having babies. I do love my mother, and while I am not by any means close with her I know she loves me too. And I truly believe she did the best she could. My sister finished raising my youngest brother from around age twelve, and my other brother now has a baby of his own. We are all doing the best we can with the cards we were dealt, and their stories are their own to tell.

While I still hold a gold medal in the Fucked-Up Family Olympics, I have managed to live a pretty normal life. And although I didn't become a doctor or the first woman in the NFL, I think one of the great miracles of my story is that I didn't end up dead in an alley with a needle sticking out of my arm. I know a few people who did.

I dropped out of college and eventually went to beauty school. I am a licensed cosmetologist in the state of Colorado. I own and operate my own salon studio. I've been my own boss for quite some time now, and life is good. I have a tall, handsome husband who is pretty decent to me, and two beautiful children. I always joke that my childhood was a mix between *Shameless* and *8 Mile*. And yet somehow, I've managed to climb my way into the middle-class. I have a Jack Russell rescue that pees on everything, two cats who hate me and have been living the American Dream, or my milfy suburban version of it for quite some time now.

My love and gratitude for my mother's family is exponential. I will be forever grateful for the positive impact they have had on my life. My grandfather in particular showed me a deep, loving kindness that has stuck with me long after his passing. It was always my wish to have him walk me down the aisle on my wedding day. Sadly, he passed of cancer the year before I was married. My sweet grandmother gave me his favorite pair of cowboy boots, and I wore them under my wedding dress as I walked down the aisle with my aunt. I truly believe he was there with us that day. I saved his last bag of pipe tobacco and on bad days, I open it and take a whiff to remind myself he's always with me. I named my beautiful daughter after my beloved great-grandmother. I still love Celine Dion and Eminem, and have come to accept that Lance Bass is not my one true love.

To anyone out there who can relate to this story, you are not alone. Life can be a good many things and there is a lot that is outside of our control. What we can control is the way we show up for ourselves and others in this world. I had a chip on my shoulder for a long time about the cards I was dealt, and honestly still have days where I do. And while I'm always down to pop off to any Karens I encounter in the wild, I've come to realize that we never really know what someone is going through. When someone used to cut me off in traffic, old A. J. would have flipped them the bird and been ready to throw hands at the next red light. Today, however, I try to always imagine that they just got a phone call their mother is dying in the hospital and they've got places to be faster than I do. I used to think nothing in this life was free, especially for girls like me. But it's taken me a while to realize that kindness is always free. I know, vomit, right? It's true, though.

One of the most surprising forms of healing I have found was becoming a mother myself. I work every day to give my children the childhood I wished I had had. My little Grinch heart grows every time my sweet babies tell me they love me or when they need something and I am able to buy it for them. I host all the playdates. I bake all the cookies. And I show up. Motherhood has been the wildest ride. I was scared to have children for a long time, because I was convinced I was too fucked up to do it. But my children are the greatest gifts life has given me, and I cannot wait to see what they become.

When I see fathers with their daughters in public being cute as shit, I still feel a twinge of jealously. When my friends talk about calling their dads when they need help, I am sometimes overcome with a longing for a life that didn't entail having drug-addicted, alcoholic parents. And I do wonder what that life would have looked like for me. When I pick my kids up from school and see dads show up and be there for their children, it often activates a dark self-pitying corner of my soul. However, I've discovered that healing from my trauma has opened what seems like an unending well of strength within myself. There's not much I'm afraid of anymore. And I have an incredible ability to set boundaries with people and zero tolerance for disrespect. And although these traits have been both strengths and weaknesses in my life, I am incredibly proud of how far I have come.

I won't lie, I still have not found forgiveness in my heart for my father. After a couple glasses of red wine, I'll sometimes toss around the idea of having a seance to make contact just so I can tell him to go fuck himself. That is something I hope I will be able to find within myself someday. The good news is I am not a ninety-year old woman relaying her memoir to one of her perfect grandchildren sitting on a beautiful front porch, peeling an orange, about to take a cinematic last breath. I am a thirty-two-year-old wife and mother in the trenches of life with young children. Sometimes I drink too much wine. Sometimes I do enjoy telling a douchey stranger to kick rocks. I sleep with my makeup on. I never floss. Sometimes I ice my husband and friends out for no reason. And while none of us can know how many years we have left, I know I am a work in progress. I have more growing and healing to do. But this is where I'm at right here, right now.

Therapy has helped me in more ways than I can list. I strongly recommend it for everyone, no matter where you are in life. I am so happy our society is moving in a direction where we are removing the stigma associated with mental health issues. Humans are messy creatures. And now more than ever, I believe it's important to find more common ground with our fellow man. Honestly, I'm shaking my head while writing this. Hood rat A. J. would have slapped the shit out of me for even thinking that. But I am so grateful for the kindness and beauty I have found in this world. We have more in common with the strangers beside us than we think.

And to all those who had a childhood like mine, I am truly sorry you went through whatever you did. You didn't deserve it. It wasn't fair. But because of it, you have more strength inside you than you know. Harness it. Hone it. And stop waiting for Prince Charming to come sweep you off your feet. Sometimes you have to be your own superhero.

Acknowledgments

This book is an explosion of thirty-two years of pent-up rage, family secrets, and a long journey of healing, all coming to a head. I sat down at my computer one day, burnt out on motherhood, wallowing in self-loathing and depression, and decided to put my story on paper. A lot of people helped me find my voice throughout this process, and I would like to give credit where credit is due.

My siblings lived this trauma with me, and we were silent partners, bonded through mutual misery for a time. I have always loved you and wished nothing but the best for you. I wish you a lifetime of happiness and healing. And to my sister in particular, you assumed the role of a parent at a young age, providing me guidance and support. For a long time, I thought we were too different to ever find common ground. Little did I know, we've had common ground this whole time. I thank you for encouraging me to tell this story. You're a boss-ass bitch, Shannon. Don't ever forget that.

To my unofficial editor and bestie, Kate; I thank you for your unwavering support and diligence. Your words of encouragement and attention to detail continue to challenge me to strive for greatness, long after the completion of this project. I only hope to repay the favor with your own writing. Thank you for visiting me on your lunch breaks and listening to my rants about stupid shit. I appreciate you more than you'll ever know.

To my other unofficial editor and sweet auntie, Julia; I thank you for your time. From the very inception of this idea, you have been my hype woman. You have read all the garbage I sent you and built me up every step of the way. You taught me how to dig deeper. You taught me how to see the beauty in the process. You may never know how much it means to me that you of all people always make time for me. I have such a profound respect for you as a woman and a mother. Thank you for being a real one.

To my beautiful Aunt Denise, the queen of research. I thank you for your time as well and always taking my calls. Thank you for your endless depths of wisdom and love. Your ability to gather information has helped me more than you know. Thank you for tying up loose ends and separating family lore and legend from reality. Thank you for reading my edits, despite your busy life, and giving me a real and beautiful example of what being a mother is.

To Stephy, my bestie; thank you for the late nights, the long talks, and the fierceness of your friendship. Thank you for saying yes every time I asked you to drink with me at noon and bounce my book ideas off of you. Thank you for watching my sweet babies. I know I have the emotional range of a Cheez-It, but I do so admire your ability to wear your heart on your sleeve. You have a beautiful soul. Thank you for sharing it with me.

To my husband, Josh; thank you for your patience during this process. I know I've been distant and messy through it all, and I appreciate the ones you took for the team. You're a good man and no matter what this life brings us, I will always value your love, friendship, and the lessons you have taught me. I love you to the moon, Joshy. Let's go have some drinks out of coconuts.

To my son, Oliver; your brilliance is unparalleled. You were too young to read this while I was writing it, but I did appreciate you trying to read it even after I told you not to. I do know you could have helped me make it even better. Keep pushing boundaries and challenging the norm. You are so special, and I will be forever grateful that I was lucky enough to be your mama. Always remember that this life is what you make it. You're going places, kid. I love you.

To my daughter, Iva, you sweet little princess. Your sass and elegance are the eighth wonder of this world. Thank you for always challenging and inspiring me. Your silly spirit and resilience continue to uplift me. I know one day you'll be the one I'm looking up to. I love you, my sweet little biscuit.

To my writing club; look at me now, bitches! Thank you for the red wine and unending well of inspiration. To Susannah in particular, I have never met someone quite like you. Your ability to see the potential in every human, even when I thought they were garbage, is beautiful. Thank you for the edits, encouragement, and shenanigans.

To Mrs. Vick, my fourth-grade English teacher, for igniting a passion within me for a good story. And most importantly, for teaching me how to tell one. I will be forever grateful for your incessant hounding over proper grammar and correct use of "your" and "you're." I hope wherever you are, it is full of proper grammar and happiness.